JESUS IS
SHALOM

JESUS IS
SHALOM

A Vision of Peace from the Gospels

Joseph A. Grassi

Paulist Press
New York/Mahwah, N.J.

Cover design by Sharyn Banks
Book design by Lynn Else

Cover art: Jean-Baptiste de Champaigne, *Sermon on the Mount*
Photo courtesy of Réunion des Musées Nationaux / Art Resource, NY

Library of Congress Cataloging-in-Publication Data

Grassi, Joseph A.
Jesus is shalom : a vision of peace from the Gospels / Joseph A. Grassi.
    p. cm.
Includes bibliographical references.
ISBN 0-8091-4308-9 (alk. paper)
1. Peace—Religious aspects—Christianity. 2. Bible. N.T. Gospels—Criticism, interpretation, etc. I. Title.
BS2555.6.P5G73 2006
261.8′73—dc22

                                                                2005019713

Published by Paulist Press
997 Macarthur Boulevard
Mahwah, New Jersey 07430

www.paulistpress.com

Printed and bound in the
United States of America

CONTENTS

INTRODUCTION

"Peace, peace when there is no peace" (Jer 6:14). With these words the prophet Jeremiah complained about the deceptive meaning of peace in his day, more than 500 years before the birth of Jesus. Government and military leaders in Jeremiah's day continually emphasized that "peace" meant security and safety through their plans for military solutions guaranteed by God's blessing. God, however, told Jeremiah that true peace could only come through a return to the covenant of peace and justice that God had given his people. A copy of this covenant written in stone was kept in the Holy of Holies of the Temple. Jeremiah's message was a dangerous one, even as it is today. He was beaten and put into prison for daring to confront the authorities.

This book studies the true meaning of peace found in the New Testament documents. This biblical peace differs greatly from the definitions of *peace* commonly found in the dictionary. The New Testament reveals that there was a struggle between the true and deceptive meanings of peace around Jesus' time and afterward. For example, the angels at Jesus' birth announced a joyful message of "peace on earth." Yet Jesus later warned, "Do not think that I have come to bring 'peace on earth' but rather division" (Luke 12:51). Jesus had in mind the false slogan of "peace on earth" proclaimed by the Roman military under the name of Pax Romana. Its purpose was to control the world to promote Roman domination, business, and wealth. Fear was Rome's greatest weapon, and "peace and security" were promised to the masses to maintain order and provide protection from "freedom fighters" and "terrorists."

The challenge presented to the world by the gospels and St. Paul is the image of Jesus, a Messiah of peace and nonviolence—an image that involves serious decisions and challenges to daily lifestyle and the world we live in. Peace can only be understood

1

from the full image and meaning of *shalom* as found in the Hebrew Bible and the four gospels. This shalom has a deep religious meaning as flowing from God and only obtained by prayer, commitment to God, and effective action. This is the rationale behind the title, *Jesus Is Shalom*. In this book, we will study this image along with the practical responses to it that Jesus asks of those who are his true disciples. Here we will find the hope and encouragement needed so much to transform our own lives and the violent atmosphere of so much of the world around us.

THE BIBLICAL MEANING OF SHALOM: A BRIEF PRIMER OF PEACE

Shalom has even found a place in the English dictionary, which briefly notes that it is Hebrew meaning "peace" and that it is used in greetings and farewells. However, *shalom* in the Bible is not the same as "peace" in English. It has a distinct religious value and a wide variety of meanings depending on the context. Yet, basic to all these meanings is a remarkable view that the ancients had of an interconnected, energy-filled world. To understand this better, we will make some analogies with modern scientific views.

Modern and Ancient Views of the Universe

Every schoolchild soon learns the famous formula of Einstein, $E = MC^2$. This tells us that energy is interconvertible with mass. Our senses only perceive the outward forms that this inner energy assumes. That is, unless it escapes through an atomic explosion! Then it could wipe out whole populations. On earth, most of our energies come from atomic explosions on the sun. Some of them are so harmful they could kill us were it not for a protective screen miles thick provided by our atmosphere. Yet even with this protection, looking at the sun for just a few moments could blind us for life, even though it is 92 million miles away.

Despite these tremendous energies, there are common building blocks for all the materials in the universe. Every school has posted atomic tables with the names of all the elements along with the configurations of electrons and other particles that make up each one. However, what we know mainly through our minds and intellects, the ancients perceived instinctively. For them, the world was filled with energies they called *dynameis* in the Greek world—some were good and others were harmful.

In regard to life itself, you readers belong to the first generation in millions of years of history to possess the greatest intellectual knowledge ever gained by the human race. This is the discovery that all living creatures have a basic oneness at their essence and contain the same mutually understandable language in their genes. There is a special kinship and relationship among the animal, plant, and human world that was never known until now. For example, our closest animal relative, the chimpanzee, has 98 percent of its genes in common with us. Even a common rat shares more than 90 percent of its genes with humans.

We now know that the cells of all living creatures on earth have a common language that is used by all the genes. This collection, called the genome, is a book of stories. Our biblical ancestors knew nothing from this scientific standpoint but perceived it intuitively. The world of biblical shalom was alive and dynamic with a harmony and intercommunion among all creatures, great and small. It was like a living Internet or Web where each individual act reverberated on all and affected all. The Internet today depends on sources of energy we call "servers." Without them, it all falls apart. However, for the ancients, each person was a "server" because of the Spirit they felt and experienced within every creature.

Nevertheless, there are great contrasts between the modern and ancient biblical worldview. The latter was based on what could be known from the five senses. There was no concept of outer space, farther than this earth and the sky. The visible stars were like chandeliers hanging from the sky. The sky itself was like a large transparent dome used for a modern sports arena. The dome was supported by the mountain pillars at its lower edge. The sun had its bedchamber at one end, rose up and traveled across the sky and "back to bed" again. The earth floated on waters below it. There was also water above the dome, as "proved" by the blue sky and the rain that poured down. Above all of this was God's throne, from which, with the help of numerous angel assistants, he governed and coordinated everything below.

The story of creation in the first chapter of Genesis presents the harmony and connectivity in this universe. For example, the movement of the moon, sun, and "stars" were signs for the seasons, days and years, feasts, planting and harvest (1:14). At the same time, there were certain powers of chaos right from the beginning (1:1–2) that occasionally erupted and had to be kept in check. The earthquakes, floods, drought, hurricanes, and other disasters came from the powers of chaos. But all in all, peoples' lives went on in relative harmony. At the end of creation, "God saw everything that he had made and indeed it was very good." It was a complete and finished work, so "on the seventh day, God finished the work that he had done, and he rested on the seventh day" (2:2).

Meanings of Shalom—Examples from a Wide Range of Usage

The word *peace* is found some 165 times in the Hebrew Bible, but indirect references to the word many times more. The verb root *shalam* follows the world image of wholeness, finishing, or completeness. For example, "All the work that King Solomon did on the house of the LORD was finished" (1 Kgs 7:51). In fact there is likely a deliberate parallel in sounds between the common SLM consonants in the Hebrew words *shalom*, "finish," and *Solomon*.

The cognate verb or noun *shalem* brings out the dimension of perfection or fullness. For example, King Solomon addressed the people with these words, "Let your heart be *perfect* before the LORD our God to walk in his statutes and to keep his commandments" (1 Kgs 8:61, literally). In giving this and other examples, sometimes the same meaning may be conveyed by a parallel word, for example, *tom*, Hebrew for "perfect." The Qumran Community near the

Jordan River called themselves a community of the "perfect" because they made an additional vow to share their possessions.

The prominent area of peace was that of "covenant," found some 300 times in the Hebrew Bible. There were covenants with individuals, families, nations, and above all with God as the supreme *covenant of peace*. God declares through Isaiah: "For the mountains may depart and the hills be removed, but my steadfast love shall not depart from you, and my *covenant of peace* shall not be removed, says the LORD, who has compassion on you (54:10). The motives for this covenant are God's "steadfast love," a translation of *chesed*, a contractual love, and *rachum*, a womb-compassionate love. For individual relationships, a close friend was "a person of my peace." David laments that even the "man of my shalom, in whom I trusted, has lifted his heel against me" (Ps 41:9). Jesus quotes this verse at the Last Supper to describe Judas, one of the Twelve and a close friend who was about to betray him (John 13:18).

However, unlike God, no human being is ever perfect in keeping covenants of peace. So they needed to continually renew and refresh them. This was done with a sacrifice called a *shelem*, a peace offering. These are mentioned 85 times in the Bible, usually on some joyful occasion. Everyday there was a peace offering in the Temple, with increased numbers on feasts and private occasions. They were not only community offerings but were also used to cement relationships. In view of the world Internet type of relationships with one another and with God, the lifeblood of the animal was given to God, then part of the peace offering to a priest, and the rest was shared in a banquet with others. Meat was a delicacy, so the animal was especially raised for such festive occasions. There was no intention of slaughter for its own sake.

God and Shalom

Peace is not merely a quality or attribute of God, but belongs to his essence as the continuous creative energy behind an interconnected universe. On one occasion, God is identified with peace when Gideon, a judge of Israel, built an altar and called it "The LORD is peace" (Judg 6:24). Human beings by their own efforts cannot reach true peace, but God can share it with them.

The way he does this is usually through a blessing, which is a communication of divine energy. Originally, God gave only the high priest the right to convey God's blessing of peace. However, after the destruction of the Temple, it became more commonly used in the synagogue and in homes. It was believed to have the special power of healing the sick. The words to be used, according to God's instructions were: "The LORD bless you and keep you; the LORD make his face to shine upon you, and be gracious to you; the LORD lift up his countenance upon you, and give you *peace*." Then God said to Moses, "So they shall put my name on the Israelites, and I will bless them" (Num 6:24–27). It was customary for people to bow their heads at each of the three invocations of LORD, for the communication of power came from this name of names.

Because peace is a gift that can only come from God, the psalms frequently echo invocations for peace. Notable is Psalm 122 with its triple plea for peace beginning with verse six, "Pray for the *peace* of Jerusalem: May they prosper who love you. *Peace* be within your walls, and security within your towers. For the sake of my relatives and friends I will say, '*Peace* be within you.'" The psalm has a musical play on words with the similar sounding *shalom* and the Hebrew ending *shalem* of Jerusalem.

Peace, Justice, and Joy

Peace and justice are like twins who always go together. The psalmist sings, "Justice and peace will kiss each other" (85:10). Or they may be in poetic parallel: In regard to those who are evil, "The way of peace they do not know and there is no justice in their paths" (Isa 59:8). However, peace is more like the state that results from works of justice: "The effect of justice will be peace, and the result of justice, quietness and trust forever" (Isa 32:17). This quietness and unending trust is also a description of peace.

Peace and joy also are often found together. The God of shalom is a God of joy. "Joy" or "joyful" is found around 250 times in the Bible. One beautiful text of peace and joy is found in Isaiah 55:12: "For you shall go out in joy, and be led back in peace; the mountains and the hills before you shall burst into song, and all the trees of the field shall clap their hands." We notice how all nature joins in this joy in the prophets and psalms: The mountains dance and sing, the trees clap their hands.

Messianic Hopes for Peace

These are based on the promises God made to David the king about a glorious future for his offspring, especially in regard to peace and justice (2 Sam 7:12–15). God's covenant with the people will be mediated by the Davidic kings. Isaiah declared, "A child has been born for us, a son given to us; authority rests upon his shoulders; and he is named Wonderful Counselor, Mighty God, Everlasting Father, *Prince of Peace.* His authority shall grow continually, and there shall be endless *peace* for the throne of David and his kingdom. He will establish and uphold it with justice and with righteousness from this time onward and forevermore. The zeal of the LORD of hosts will do this" (9:6–7). The same prophet draws an image of this peace from the Garden of Eden when all of nature was in harmony: "The wolf shall live with the lamb, the leopard shall lie down with the kid, the calf and the lion and the fatling together, and a little child shall lead them." (11:6).

Peace and the Fullness of the Good Things of the Earth

The full dimensions of peace include enjoying all the good things this earth provides, including many children, good health, food, trees, plants, and animals. God will ensure that the rains come in their season, the crops yield their produce, the trees yield their fruits, the threshing and vintage overtake one another, an abundance of bread be provided, good health and protection from enemies and wild animals be assured. Such is the description in Leviticus, ending with the words, "I will grant peace in the land and you shall lie down and no one shall make you afraid" (26:3–6).

Greetings of Shalom

All the above benefits of a complete and harmonious world are included in the common greeting: "Peace be to you." This is not the granting of peace to another. It is really a prayer that God will grant peace, for he alone is the author of peace. Thus the words carry the divine energy and presence. The common words of departure were "Go in peace." This is a command or dismissal that sends people away with divine protection and guidance on their journey. Since the power of life and death was in God's hands, one must also have a dismissal in order to go on the journey to death. So Simeon can finally say to God, "Now you are dismissing your servant in peace" after he had seen the child Jesus in the Temple (Luke 2:29).

True and False Shalom

The prophet Jeremiah inveighed against false prophets and priests who proclaimed a peace that was deceptive and false: "They have treated the wound of my people carelessly, saying, 'Peace, peace,' when there is no peace" (6:14). This false peace was promoted by government and religious leaders who trusted in military solutions rather than the true peace found in the covenant of peace that God had made with his people. This false peace proclaimed that God would bless them and protect them through his presence in the Temple, even though the people did not follow God's covenant that was within the Temple. Jeremiah responded in these words, "Thus says the LORD of hosts, the God of Israel: 'Amend your ways and your doings, and let me dwell with you in this place. Do not trust in these deceptive words: 'This is the temple of the LORD, the temple of the LORD, the temple of the LORD'" (Jer 7:4–5).

Then follow the conditions under which God could dwell with his people, which are essentially the ancient core of the covenant: "For if you truly amend your ways and your doings, if you truly act justly one with another, if you do not oppress the alien, the orphan, and the widow, or shed innocent blood in this place, and if you do not go after other gods to your own hurt, then I will dwell with you in this place" (Jer 7:6–7).

The Worst Enemy of Shalom

Shalom, we have seen, in its fullest sense embraces the totality and harmony of all life. So only God can actually be called shalom. This shalom is an active energy that emerges from peace-makers as children of God and flows into friends, family, nations, and even the whole world. There are many obstacles to shalom: strife, anger, insults, lies, quarrels, fights, and wars. However, the worst enemy of shalom is one that is named within the heart of God's covenant of peace. This is found in the summary of the covenant in Jeremiah, which we have quoted in the paragraph above: *those who shed innocent blood*. See also the summary in Ezekiel 18:10–13.

The Biblical Trail of Innocent Blood and Its Effects

In the Bible, a violent person who sheds innocent blood is often called "a man of blood." The very opposite of this would be a person of peace, innocence, and nonviolence. This title is not attributed to any human being in the Bible since no one but God can be completely peace. However, a close friend could be called "a person of my peace" (Ps 41:9). Jewish and Christian tradition regarded the story of Cain and Abel and those who imitated them as primary examples and even activating forces for these two opposite paths. For example, the author of the First Letter of John writes, "We must not be like Cain who was from the evil one, and murdered his brother. And why did he murder him? Because his own deeds were evil and his brother's righteous" (3:12).

This story is one of the most horrendous in the entire Bible. It occurs right after the broken peace of the Garden of Eden. It happens within the very first family in the Bible. Some details in the story of the two brothers highlight the contrasts between them. Cain was the older and Abel the younger of the two sons of Eve. No biblical genealogy is found for Abel. It is likely he was too young. He had the typical job for children, that of tending sheep, like King David as a boy. Each brother offered his gifts to God. Abel offered some young lambs; Cain as a farmer offered the first-fruits of the land. Everything seemed to prosper for Abel, but not so for Cain, who presumed that God was favoring Abel. The story notes that "Cain was very angry and his countenance fell" (4:5). He kept nursing that anger within until one day when they were alone in the fields, "Cain rose up against his brother Abel and killed him." God asked him, "Where is your brother Abel?" Cain answered, "I don't know. Am I my brother's keeper?" The narrator highlights the word *brother* in the story, repeating it seven times to bring out the sense of responsibility.

Then God describes the terrible effects of this sin on all of creation: What one person does affects *all* creation. God said to Cain, "What have you done? Listen, your brother's blood is crying out to me from the ground and now you are cursed from the ground which has opened its mouth to receive your brother's blood from your hand. When you till the earth it will no longer yield to you its strength; you will be a fugitive and a wanderer on earth" (4:12).

So we have two paths going through the Bible. Abel and Cain are not mythical figures from the past but continual archetypes of the contrast between innocent, nonviolent people and guilty people of blood and violence. Jewish and Christian tradition regards the voice of Abel's blood crying from the ground as still continuing. For example, the New Testament Letter to the Hebrews declares, "He [Abel] died but through it *he still speaks*" (11:4). And again, like Jesus, Abel made an offering of his blood: "You have come to Jesus, mediator of a new covenant, and to the sprinkled blood that *speaks* a better word than the blood of Abel" (12:24).

This innocent blood is not crying out in vain. God hears the voice of Abel, especially of innocent children like him, and responds. The earth also continues its revulsion. God's intervention in hearing the voice of a little one appears in the story of the Pharaoh of Egypt who ordered all newborn Hebrew boys thrown into the Nile. In disobedience, a mother hid her baby as long as possible but then put her little child in a protected basket by the Nile. Pharaoh's daughter came down to the river to bathe and heard the child crying and rescued him. She adopted the boy and called him *Moshe* because he was taken out, *moshah*, of the water (Exod 2:10).

Jesus also recalled the blood of the "just Abel" as part of a trail of innocent blood to which God always responds (Matt 23:35). The Book of Revelation describes the opening of the fifth seal of God's plan through history. Under (and part) of the altar of sacrifice are the souls of all those who had been slaughtered and had borne witness to God's word. Their voices cry out to God for response. They are told it will be given at God's appointed time (6:9). The voices of shalom, innocence, and nonviolence have priority with God and a power of their own that can never be overcome. Violent "men of blood" often win in the short run, but the shalom of God is always stronger in time. Shalom is forever and is mediated through the little workers like Abel.

Shalom and Forgiveness

Within the Ark of the Covenant, the stone tablets of the Torah were originally kept. They were a sign of God's covenant of peace with his people. Yet, given human weakness, it was a covenant that God had to renew often with forgiveness because the people broke it. The Israelites soon broke the original covenant on Sinai by worship of the golden calf (Exod 32:1–10). Yet knowing God's mercy, Moses begged for the people's forgiveness (32:32). The basis for this forgiveness was the meaning of God's revelation name that he showed to Moses, a God who kept his covenant love "for a thousand generations, forgiving iniquity, transgression, and sin" (34:7). So this forgiveness was repeated again and again.

Even centuries later, Nehemiah prayed, "You are a God ready to forgive, gracious and merciful, slow to anger and abounding in steadfast love" (9:17). Promises for a future with a new covenant always included the promise of even more generous forgiveness. God told Jeremiah that the days were coming when he would make a new covenant in which the law of God would be written on peoples' hearts. In this covenant, God said, "I will forgive their iniquity and remember their sin no more" (31:31–34).

This chapter only presents the broad outlines of the meaning of *shalom* in the Bible—what Christians often call the Old Testament. Yet it is really never antiquated but ever renewed. The following chapters uncover the meaning of *shalom* in basic texts of the four gospels.

2

THE GOSPEL OF MARK: BUILDING A NEW WORLD PEACE TEMPLE

"My house shall be called a house of prayer for all the nations"
(Mark 11:17)

The Old and New Temple

The word *peace* is most often used in small circles, such as in greetings, covenants, and reconciliations. However, we have seen in the last chapter that it once had much larger dimensions. In its meaning of harmony and wholeness it referred to nations and even to the whole known Roman world at the time of Mark. Harmony required the breakdown of barriers, and the greatest for Mark was that between Jews and non-Jews, called "Gentiles." All visitors to the Temple area knew this in a very visual and tactile manner. There was actually a three-foot high barrier in the Temple court with a notice warning Gentiles not to go any farther under pain of death. Parts of this inscription have been found. The preeminent Gentiles of course were the Roman occupation army and its personnel in Israel.

Mark wrote his Gospel during or shortly after the end of the Roman war with Israel, between AD 67 and 71. The Temple was destroyed around AD 70. This was a crushing blow for the Jewish people. The Temple building originally contained the Ark of the

Covenant with its two stone tablets guaranteeing God's covenant with his people and their unique access to him. When the Temple was destroyed, people knew this was not an event outside of God's power and plans. Somehow, God would be with them regardless. Jesus had predicted the destruction of the Temple (13:2). Other prophets like Jeremiah (7:1–15) had done so, insisting this would happen if the people did not keep the covenant that gave the whole meaning to the Temple.

However, Jesus also promised he would build a *new* Temple—but not a material structure—as a place where all nations, those of Jewish origin as well as Gentiles, could come together in peace. We have called this a "peace temple" because the very core of the Temple was the Ark of the Covenant holding the stone tablets of covenant that God had made with his people. This was called a "covenant of peace" that God had given to Israel (Ezek 34:25; 37:26).

Jesus' design became evident during his last visit to Jerusalem, his cleansing of the Temple, and especially at his death. Only then, a Roman centurion, in an attitude of worship, proclaimed him to be God's son (15:39). This symbolized the breakdown of the ancient world barrier to peace. The whole Gospel moves toward this point, so we must trace this process from the beginning. However, to understand this better we need a picture of Mark's audience and their situation.

Mark's Audience Under Intense Roman Oppression

As for the Gospel audience, Mark has to explain Jesus' customs and beliefs, for example, about washing hands (7:3–4), the Passover lamb (14:12), the preparation day for the Sabbath (15:42). He translates Aramaic words and phrases (see 3:17; 5:41; 7:11, 34; 15:22, 34). This indicates an audience more likely to include a majority of Gentile converts, although there were also Jewish converts as well. As for the community atmosphere, there were two pressing concerns: (1) intense Roman oppression and persecution, along with (2) the recent destruction of the Jewish Temple.

All this suffering led to serious questions among believers. What does it all accomplish? What good does it do? Does it make a real difference in their effort to bring Romans into their faith? Many believers surely felt that Jesus' last words on the cross were really their own cry, "My God, my God, why have you forsaken me?" (15:34). As answers to these questions, some Christian prophets were teaching that the Temple destruction was a great act of God as a prelude to Christ's return in power. They claimed that this return was already being heralded by signs and wonders. Mark has Jesus warn against these prophets with words like these: "Many will come in my name and say, 'I am he' and they will lead many astray" (13:6). Jesus also says, "False messiahs and false prophets will appear and produce signs and omens to lead astray, if possible, the elect" (13:22).

To respond to these prophets of a powerful messiah, Jesus first of all announces that no definite predictions can be made about his imminent return. He tells the audience, "About that day or hour, no one knows, neither the angels in heaven, nor the Son, but only the Father" (13:32). The local destruction of the Temple is *not* an imminent sign of his return. In contrast, his return will be accompanied by universal signs: The Son of Man will come in the clouds in great power and gather his elect from the four winds from the end of the earth to the end of heaven (13:26–27). As to when this will happen, the suffering and witness of faithful believers will make it all possible: They will stand before governors and kings for Jesus' sake to bear witness, *martyrion*, to them, "The good news must first be proclaimed before all the nations" (13:9–10). In other words, the suffering of believers will be changed into a positive achievement in preaching the gospel to all nations.

The Way of Jesus as Effective Witness to the World

The Baptism Scene by the Jordan

To effectively bear witness to the world, what will most impress the world? Mark writes his Gospel to outline an effective way to live in imitation of Jesus. It all starts in a wilderness area near the Jordan River. When the people of Israel first crossed that river it meant for them a transition into a new era and a new life. People left even faraway homes to come down to listen to John and be baptized by him. "John the baptizer appeared in the wilderness, proclaiming a baptism of repentance for the forgiveness of sins" (1:4). As a result, people from the whole region came to him and they were baptized by him in the river Jordan, confessing their sins.

What made John so effective and attractive? First of all, he was convinced that he was a chosen messenger of God, a channel through whom God spoke and acted. He was a man of destiny, fulfilling a great plan of history written in the books of God's prophets. God had said to Isaiah, "See, I am sending my messenger ahead of you, who will prepare your way" (1:2). What was the message of God that the Baptist brought? It was very simple: "The time is fulfilled, and the kingdom of God is at hand; repent and believe in the good news" (1:15, where it is repeated by Jesus).

The command of God was *repentance*. People knew this was the essence of the prophetic message over the ages. Isaiah is the favorite prophet of Mark, whom he quotes more often than any other gospel. Isaiah cites God's word: "Wash yourselves; make yourselves clean; remove the evil of your doings from before my eyes; cease to do evil, learn to do good; seek justice, rescue the oppressed, defend the orphan, plead for the widow" (1:16–17). The orphan, the widow, and the oppressed were usually the landless with no one to provide for them.

The Baptism and Call of Jesus

Jesus made a long journey of some three days to come all the way from Nazareth in Galilee to the Jordan River in Judea. John's reputation had reached far and wide. Jesus as a young man was looking for new guidance for his future. At the Jordan, under John's guidance, he plunged himself into the water along with people from all over Judea who were confessing their sins and asking for forgiveness. Just as Jesus was coming out of the water, he saw a dove, a symbol of the Spirit, descend upon him. Then he heard God's voice speaking to him alone (in Mark's Gospel) with the words, "You are my son the beloved, with whom I am well pleased" (1:11).

These words are taken from several scripture passages, most importantly, Psalm 2, which relates the opposition of earthly kings to God's chosen anointed king, his *Messiah* in Hebrew, his *Christos* in Greek. This was the title given to an ideal future king and son of David who would fulfill God's hopes for the people and nation. In this psalm, God decrees that a son of David will be "my king" and declares, "You are my son" (2:6–7). This phrase is an adoption formula for kings, especially David, in the Bible (2 Sam 7:14; Ps 89:26–27). Jesus and the Gospel audience would have known the full meaning of "You are my son." Connected with a son of David are all the titles and promises of peace we find in Isaiah. For example, he shall be called "Prince of Peace" (9:6) and there will be "endless peace for the throne of David and his kingdom" (9:7).

The implications of this baptismal revelation become Jesus' secret in this Gospel. It will only be fully understood at the cross. There, with the inscription, "King of the Jews," over Jesus' head, a Roman centurion, a hardened specialist in cruel executions, announces, "Truly this man was God's son." Mark makes this confession a parallel to God's voice at Jesus' baptism. The centurion symbolizes Rome and its power over the world. True peace and harmony in the world will only come through the cross, which sums up Jesus' suffering and death. Jesus' baptism is a model for the baptism of believers. They must follow Jesus all the way to the cross if they are to be his instruments of peace in the world.

Jesus' Temptation and Struggle with Satan (1:14–15)

Serious decisions for all come after baptism, and this is true of Jesus as a model for the struggle with temptation. When an inner call comes from God, like that of Jesus, it involves difficult choices, for that is what temptation means. Satan is the embodiment of all the powers of evil in the world that people must face. The story is brief at this point because the whole Gospel is Jesus' story of courageous conflict with evil. Yet evil is not simply a disaster but a test, opportunity, and challenge to respond and overcome through the tremendous power of the Spirit within. Not to respond—or to remain neutral—is to cooperate in evil.

Mark describes the result of Jesus' serious choices. Jesus at first decided to stay with the small community of John's disciples near the Jordan. But then another serious decision faced him. John, his teacher, was arrested by Herod. This resulted from John's courageous stand in confronting Herod's moral injustice (see particulars in 6:17–29). As a colleague of John, Jesus felt the shadow of imprisonment and death fall upon him if he continued John's work of preaching. Despite this, he went bravely ahead. In fact, God's message was so important and urgent for him that Jesus took the ultimate risk by going *beyond* the teacher John. He left the narrow valley of the Jordan and went up to Galilee to reach a broader public. John had waited for people to come down to him in repentance. Jesus, in contrast, took the initiative to go to people where they were and invite them even at home or at their work. Jesus' first recorded words, the perennial message of God addressed to readers, were "The time is fulfilled and the kingdom of God has come near; repent and believe in the good news" (1:14–15).

The Call of the First Disciples and Those of Any Time (1:16–20)

Simon, Andrew, James, and John are examples for a gospel audience at any time. Jesus tells them and the audience, "Follow me and I will make *you* fish for people." In other words, the mission is really to change the world and bring people to God. This seems so impossible and overpowering that Jesus emphasizes that not human strength but he alone will make it possible: "*I* will make you fish for people." However, changing others only takes place when they are changed first, so the disciples left their fishing nets (which was all they had) and followed him. This does not mean giving up a means of livelihood—although it may mean so for a time—as it did for the first apostles. It *does* require a total priority for the kingdom of God that Jesus preached (1:15). This "kingdom" is a world where God truly rules, a world of peace, justice, and love. The call has priority over family, friends, and careers.

Exorcisms and Power over Evil Spirits (1:21–28)

The call to discipleship is dangerous and risky. Confidence is necessary to win a hard-fought battle against the overwhelming forces of evil. Thus, the Gospel assures readers of Jesus' inner power to do so, a resource that they will share also (6:7–13). The unclean spirit in the synagogue was a demon that made people "unclean." This does not mean "dirty" but a condition that disqualifies a person from taking part in certain religious rituals or community functions. In an age that did not know about germs and viruses (which are living beings!), the ancients attributed many illnesses to living organisms within, a demon that made people "unclean." It was important for the disciples to realize that Jesus has power over every outside controlling force, even those threatening the holy synagogue. So the people, the audience in the Gospel story, are amazed by Jesus' new teaching and authority.

A Miracles' Series and Path to Wholeness and Peace (1:40—5:43)

In our opening chapter on the nature of peace, we pointed out that wholeness and harmony were essential elements of peace. This was especially true of sicknesses that resulted in a loss of a person's full powers. To obtain peace and communion with the whole Gentile or Roman world, Jesus and the audience must first learn to create peace and wholeness in individuals and households. So a healing ministry is essential to Jesus' work and that of future disciples. Since peace and healing begin at home, the first healing is that of the mother-in-law of Simon. Her house had become the new home of Jesus after he was expelled from Nazareth (6:1–6).

According to custom, the mother of Simon's wife supervised the household, especially in matters of food and hospitality. The goal of a cure is restoration to normal life and work. It does not mean an X-ray-proved medical miracle. For Simon's mother-in-law, this restoration was to *serve them*, meaning her household, which now included Jesus and his hungry disciples. This story begins a cycle of stories about women in this Gospel who will later have a surprising new role. We will only take some examples from the miracle collection.

The Cleansing of the Leper (1:40–45)

Mark's Gospel intends to show that through Jesus' death he can heal the "uncleanness" of the Roman world. However, he starts by restoring the wholeness of individuals to full communion in the community. The most difficult case of all was leprosy. Leprosy was the most fearful and deadly form of ritual uncleanness. It was so powerful that it could be caught, like a contagious disease, by touching a leper. Consequently, these miserable people lived in groups outside cities, often in cemeteries (the supreme place of uncleanness), to avoid contact with others. They were very much like walking corpses shunned even by their own families. No one could touch or greet them for fear of contagion.

The crowds around Jesus drew back in horror when a leper came out of hiding and approached Jesus for a cure. Everyone was shocked to the core when Jesus stretched out his hand and touched him, thus incurring uncleanness himself according to the laws in Leviticus 13—14. Jesus commanded the man, "Be made clean!" Then he ordered the man to go to the Temple priests and perform the ceremonies necessary to reconsecrate himself for full participation once more in community life. Only this would complete the work of wholeness and peace. The message was clear that the disciples' mission was to go out to the outcasts and marginalized of the world to bring them back to full restoration. Nothing less is enough. Handouts and charity could be even demeaning without the goal of full dignity and community restoration.

Jesus commanded the man, "See that you say nothing to anyone." This sounds impossible, but Mark wants the audience to know that Jesus deliberately played down his healer role to draw attention to his teaching and the message of repentance. Just previous to this story, Jesus had risen early, while still dark, and gone off to pray. The disciples hunted him down and told him that everyone was seeking him (for cures). But Jesus replied that he was not to remain a local healer. He told them, "Let us go to the neighboring towns so that I may proclaim the message there also, for that is what I came out to do" (1:38).

Healing of the Paralytic and the Forgiveness of Sins (2:1–12)

Mark described this in such detail to illustrate that Jesus' healing was not just *external*, but a cure of the *whole* person. This involved a complete turning to God and total forgiveness of past sins. This healing and forgiving ministry of his disciples was to be a principal sign of Jesus' presence. The essential inner ingredient to make this happen lies in these words: "When Jesus saw their faith"—a trust so great that the paralytic's friends tore a hole in a thatch roof to lower him down on ropes in front of Jesus. The scribes (professional writers and religion teachers) thought that Jesus blasphemed by assuming God's authority in judgment when he said, "Son, your sins are forgiven."

Jesus replies that he has that authority on earth as *Son of Man*. This title literally means "human being." However, an audience trained in scripture would recall the great vision of the future given to the prophet Daniel (7:9–14). In that vision, God is enthroned as a judge and hands over his power and authority to one "like a Son of Man." This Son of Man is human, representing Israel, the people of God. At the same time, he is godlike, sharing God's judgment and authority. So the "Son of Man" function brings God's authority down to earth in a community of people. As Son of Man, Jesus is present in the people of God *on earth*. Therefore, the community's reception and forgiveness of others is God's own loving forgiveness as well. This removes the heavy, fearful burden of future judgment. Believers can be saved from this fear here and now. This is the meaning of "salvation," which amounts to the fullness of peace. In the Gospel ending we will see that the centurion can make his profession of faith because forgiveness is open to him.

The Test of Acceptance and Forgiveness: The Call of Levi the Tax Collector (2:1–12)

Mark's stories are closely knit together. Here we find practical application of acceptance and forgiveness for the most unlikely prospect: Levi the tax collector. Everyone despised him as an employee of an abusive Roman foreign power. Levi had become rich on the lifeblood of his own people. Yet the Master shocked everyone by choosing Levi as a disciple. Not only that, but Jesus also surprised Levi's notorious friends by welcoming them to full table fellowship with himself and his disciples. Forgiveness is not merely internal but communal as well.

The Pharisees in the story were completely shocked. These men were respected teachers of impeccable integrity. They pledged themselves to perfect observance of the traditional Law, even going beyond what the Law required. Yet Jesus answered them, "Those who are well have no need of a physician but those who are sick." As healing physician, Jesus can only help those who acknowledge they are sick and needy. Many Pharisees, as dedicated religion teachers, felt no such need. Yet Jesus stated that he had come "not to call the righteous but those who are sick." Thus the paradox: When people consider themselves righteous and good, they cannot be helped; but when they acknowledge their weakness, they become healed followers of Jesus. A most glorious title of a Christian is that of a repentant sinner.

Is Religion Serious Fasting or Joyous Feasting? (2:18–22)

Another Markan connection: In contrast to the party spirit in the previous story, the Baptist and the Pharisees followed the traditional way of repentance, which was through self-discipline, prayer, and asceticism. Jesus' way was a striking contrast. Jesus counteracted forbidden pleasures by finding *more* occasions for pleasure and joy, not fewer. So his way was like that of a joyful wedding celebration. The Jews of that time celebrated a marriage with seven full days of festivity. People put aside ordinary work and enjoyed the wine, food, and entertainment lavishly provided by the wedding party. Jesus' approach is not just a patch on an old garment (tradition); it is sparkling *new wine* that will burst any old containers (5:22).

The Joyful Spirit of the Sabbath (2:23—3:6)

The new wine motif is now applied to the holy Sabbath. The third commandment enjoined the special religious observation of every Saturday. At the end of the creation story in Genesis, "God blessed the seventh day and hallowed it because on it God rested from all the work that he had done in creation" (Gen 2:3). Rest and tranquility are closely connected to the meaning of peace. So the Sabbath is the great weekly reminder of God's covenant of peace with his people. Early Christians gradually transferred this to Sunday in memory of Jesus' resurrection. However, church leaders in time added many Sunday obligations. As these proliferated, they diminished the joy and peace of the Sabbath and made it a day of many laws and serious obligations. Jesus explained the true spirit of any law: "The Sabbath was made for humankind and not humankind for the Sabbath." True religion is person-centered not precept-centered. The Son of Man is Lord of the Sabbath. A joyful presence of the Lord makes Sunday a day of communal joy, refreshment, and peace.

In a second Sabbath story, Jesus looked at his opponents with anger. Throughout Mark, we notice that Jesus shows a full range of human emotions. Wholeness and peace come from proper expression of emotions, not repressing them, which frequently results in violence. The statements of Jesus were a real challenge to the Pharisees and others: "The Pharisees went out and immediately conspired with the Herodians against him, how to destroy him." Mark has this important plot indicator as foreshadowing the Gospel ending. Jesus' supreme independence enrages some Pharisees who feel that Jesus is subverting religious law (which was often civil law as well), thus endangering their traditions and controlled legal lifestyle. (The Herodians were supporters of King Herod, who regarded Jesus as a political threat.)

Opposition Prompts Growth, Not Failure (3:14–35)

The previous opposition of the Pharisees and others does not prompt Jesus to retreat but to advance. He appoints twelve apostles who will continue his work, even if he is forced to stop. Jesus transfers to them his unique powers to cast out demons and proclaim the message of the coming kingdom with its call for repentance (3:14). Even Jesus' family tries to restrain him, for people were saying that Jesus was out of his mind (3:21). On one occasion, Jesus' mother and brethren even tried to call him out of a crowded house where he was preaching. Jesus' response is not to do away with family support but to create an enlarged family of his disciples. Looking around at his disciples, he declared, "Whoever does the will of God is a brother and sister and a mother" (3:35).

Parables of Jesus: Hope for the Oppressed and Persecuted (4:1–34)

Mark's audience then and today have wondered whether their faithfulness has been worthwhile or unproductive when they see the limited response they receive. Their hopes for peace and a better world often seem unrealistic in face of a crescendo of evil.

Jesus was a master storyteller. A parable is really a masterpiece of art, an invitation of grace to find ourselves in the story when we compare God's ways and ours. Here, God is like a foolish farmer scattering enormous quantities of seed in places where it will be mostly lost—on a hardened path, on rocky ground, or soil covered with thorns and weeds. What a waste of time and effort this seems! Yet "other seed fell into good soil" (8). This is good, deep, receptive ground for the all-powerful seed that is the word of God (14). This yields an unbelievable harvest of "thirty and sixty and a hundredfold."

Ordinary farming at that time yielded perhaps eight or ten times as much wheat seed as that sowed. Jesus is describing a miraculous harvest only made possible by God. The biblical parallel is Isaac, the father of Jacob, when God blessed him to give him a hundredfold harvest (Gen 26:12). This occurred despite the overwhelming opposition of Isaac's enemies and a drought in the land. The seed parables follow the opposition stories to give hope to readers of all times. There will always be some deep ground in themselves, ourselves, and others to produce a miraculous harvest despite previous failures and opposition.

Mark would have smiled to know that Jesus' words have become an English proverb: "Don't hide your light under a bushel." The image was much more dramatic when using an ancient smoky oil lamp. Jesus is aware that people become very discouraged by opposition and failures. The bushel parable shows that the real failure lies in withdrawal and keeping their beautiful light/inner gifts of God to themselves. Everyone needs more encouragement to use these gifts as God's powerful light within to shine on others. If stifled, these gifts grow weaker; but if exposed and shared, they grow and become stronger.

Only Mark has this delightful, humorous, little-known parable about the sleeping farmer. You sow the powerful seed of God's word and then sleep and rise. You do absolutely nothing, yet the earth produces of itself. In Greek, this expression, "of itself," is *automatē*. The comic element becomes stronger when we discover the next activity of Jesus after the crescendo of rising opposition in the last two chapters. He takes a nice nap for himself on a boat trip amidst a storm, no less (4:38)! Sometimes this is the best tactic when difficulties seem overwhelming. Mark may have thought of Psalm 3:5, "I lie down and sleep; I wake again for the Lord sustains me." Sleep is often associated with peace in the Bible, for example, "I will both lie down and sleep in peace; for you, O LORD, make me lie down in safety" (Ps 4:8).

Next is the parable of the tiny mustard seed and the whole world (4:30–32). The tiny mustard seed can hardly be seen, yet it produces a small tree. This is a striking image of insignificant and perhaps discouraging beginnings but also of tremendous, far-reaching impact: a tree large enough that the *birds of the air* make nests in it. These birds are a biblical image of the whole world taken from the prophet Daniel (4:10–22). Because of the "Internet" effect, each person's efforts count, small as they may seem. This is especially true in the worldview of *shalom*, where the close interconnections make possible great changes through apparently small individual efforts.

Jesus Stills a Storm—Peace in Face of a Stormy World (4:35–41)

Jesus acts like Elijah, a biblical prophet in intimate communion with the forces of nature. Elijah could pray for a rainstorm and then wait for it to come (1 Kgs 18:41–45). He could also stop rainstorms (1 Kgs 19:1). However, ancient audiences found a deeper meaning from their scriptural background. In the Bible, God appears to be inattentive and sleeping during the storms and trials of life. However, an urgent prayer "wakes him up" and he responds with dramatic swift action to calm the storms (Ps 44:23–26). So the ultimate "secret weapon" in face of discouragement is to call upon Jesus when he seems to be "asleep": "Teacher, do you not care that we are perishing?" The response is immediate: Jesus awakens, takes immediate charge, and rebukes the "stormy weather" with the words, "Peace! Be still!" Only Mark has the command "peace." God is peace, and the author of peace. True lasting peace can only come from a divine source or energy.

Mark's Sense of Humor and the Drowned Pigs (5:1-21)

This is a baffling story for modern readers. Some have even accused Jesus of cruelty to animals because two thousand pigs drowned in the sea! Here again, an old key to meaning has been lost. If we saw a sign on a wall, "Down with the pigs," we would not complain to the SPCA but presume something else is indicated. The Gospel story is meant to be a humorous one—a form not immediately apparent to serious, somber readers. The old scriptural key is the biblical story where Pharaoh and his army (the Gentile pigs!) were drowned in the sea while pursuing the people of Israel (Exod 14). The Jews frequently called the Gentiles, especially the Romans, "pigs." This was because they not only ate that forbidden meat but even regarded pigs as sacred in religious ceremonies and kept them as pets.

This story is a counterpart to Jesus' first exorcism in the heart of Judaism, the synagogue. It portrays Jesus' coming victory over the demons controlling the Roman world. Their military might is symbolized by the demons' name, "Legion." The cemetery scene, the unrestrainable, naked, screeching demoniac—all symbolize the powers of death and abusive Roman power that Jesus will overcome not by *force* but by *transformation* into peaceful union. The greatest surprise comes when the former naked "streaker" changes into a calm, clothed man sitting at Jesus' feet in the attitude of a disciple. This sight was so scary and awesome that the people in this Gentile area asked Jesus to leave at this time. He did so, but not before commissioning the transformed demoniac as the first missionary to the Decapolis, ten cities with a largely Gentile population. Once again, God's power shines through most unlikely channels, a source of hope for those in the Gospel audience who fear they have little hope to transform themselves, let alone the world.

New Life and Peace in Two Women's Stories (5:21–43)

Mark's cycle of miracles reaches a climax in what amounts to a "double" resurrection story. There is also a close connection between the severe ritual uncleanness in both accounts. The imminent tragic death of the young daughter of Jairus is heartrending. She has reached the Jewish marriageable age of twelve years and is an only child (implied but made explicit in Luke 8:42). Thus, she was her parents' only hope to continue their name and memory into the future. The other woman also could never marry or have children. This was because her embarrassing affliction of continuous menstrual blood made her perpetually "unclean." It was such a powerful ritual taboo that anyone she touched or any article she handled would become unclean as well (Lev 15:25–30). We can hardly imagine a more desperate condition than that of this poor social outcast. No one could even touch or greet her with an embrace.

Mark has intertwined these two stories to present them as a teaching example of how to deal with the most impossible situation or human tragedy. We can find four steps: 1) A profound realization that all human cure seems impossible. The young girl was weak enough to be at the point of death and had already taken her last breath before Jesus arrived. The woman had gone through twelve years of agony and no doctor could help her. 2) They each approach Jesus—the girl through her father, a synagogue leader, and the other woman by sneaking up behind him in the crowd. The woman was afraid that her contagious uncleanness would lead someone, especially a religious teacher, to shun her. 3) They each had total faith and trust. Jesus later said to the woman, "Daughter, your faith has made you well." In regard to the young girl, the father does not give up despite a message that his daughter has just died but accepts Jesus' assurance, "Do not fear, but only believe." 4) Each had personal contact with Jesus. The woman trusted that even just touching his cloak would draw out the Master's healing power. For the young girl, "He [Jesus] took her by the hand and spoke to her." Mark highlights the unusual nature of this cure by noting the exact words that Jesus spoke in his own Aramaic language: *Talitha cum,*" which means "Little girl, get up!"

Mark usually omits all the peace greetings in his Gospel. But in the case of the hemorrhaging woman he notes that Jesus told her, "Go in peace and be healed of your disease." This is because this was the first touch and greeting this woman had received in twelve years. She had become *whole* once again, which is a root meaning of peace. Once more she could enjoy communion with others, marry, and have children. It was really a passage from death to life.

Shadows of the Cross—
Continuity Through Preaching and
Community Meals for All (6:14—8:21)

After the last miracle, the story of Jesus' rejection even in his hometown of Nazareth follows (6:1–6). This is a shadow of the cross, of Jesus' ultimate rejection. However, Jesus' presence and mission will carry on. He chooses twelve men with whom he shares his powers. As a result, they went out and proclaimed that all should repent (6:13). Jesus' healing ministry for the sick continues: "They anointed with oil many who were sick and cured them" (6:14).

In the next story, Herod executes Jesus' former teacher, John the Baptist, because he had the courage to stand up for the truth in face of moral decay (6:17–29). When the Twelve returned from their preaching and healing tour, they reported to Jesus all they had done. With John the Baptist dead, they must have wondered what would happen to them if Jesus faced a similar fate. Jesus then asked them to come apart and rest a while since they had been so active that they hardly had time to eat. Knowing they needed nourishment and strength, he wanted to show them how he would always provide this for them and the world. So from chapters six to eight we have the great "bread section" of the Gospel with two multiplications for five thousand and four thousand people. They are at the heart of the Gospel. Jesus could not create a new world Temple of Peace unless he provided covenant-shared meals uniting Jews and Gentiles and open to the hungry and poor.

Jesus Feeds Five Thousand People (6:30–44)

The answer to the effect of Jesus' possible death like the Baptist will be found in a new continuing presence of Jesus as shepherd and leader. The references to sheep without a shepherd, rest, and green grass point to the influence of Psalm 23, "The Lord is my shepherd." Jesus will remain with them as a nourishing shepherd. Mark brings this out through the loaves' multiplication stories. Once again, a modern audience may miss a great deal without the background of the Hebrew scriptures. There we find the theme that God multiplies bread when it is shared with others at his command. For example, a poor widow and her son shared their last bit of flour and bread with the prophet Elijah. As a result, God promised that her flour would mysteriously replenish itself as long as necessary (1 Kgs 17:8–16). Also, the prophet Elisha at God's command fed a hundred men with only twenty small pancake-shaped loaves (2 Kgs 4:42–44). As a result, they ate and were completely satisfied as the bread mysteriously multiplied.

Most important, when God gave the people of Israel the manna bread in the desert, there was always enough for everyone. This happened because God directed that everyone should go out and gather this bread, young and old, weak or strong. As a result, some gathered more and some less. However, God ordered that at the day's end, all the bread was to be equally divided with everyone to create a great miracle of sharing (Exod 16:1–36). From this experience there arose the slogan, "From each according to their ability; to each according to their need." This is not from Karl Marx but from the Bible. There is a reference to it in the early church's practice of sharing food and possession in Acts 4:35–36.

In view of the above background, when the disciples came to Jesus to present the needs of the hungry crowd, Jesus gave them the impossible command, "You give them something to eat." When the disciples naturally objected, he asked, "How many loaves have you? Go and see." After inquiring around the crowds, they found a few people willing to share the limited amount of bread they usually carried for their journeys, a meager five loaves and two fishes. "Taking the five loaves and the two fish...he blessed and broke the loaves and gave them to his disciples to set before the crowd." (These words are remarkably similar, and are likely linked, to those used by Jesus at the Last Supper.)

Jesus first has the crowd sit down on the green grass in smaller groups so sharing can more easily take place. Then he mysteriously continues sharing the bread until five thousand people are completely satisfied. It appears to be a *new bread* since twelve baskets are left over from only five loaves to start with. (These "leftovers" may be a hint that there is bread also for the audience to share!) Just as the Last Supper can only be understood in light of Jesus' death, so also the feeding narrative needs the next story. This tells how Jesus walked on water, symbolically conquering the forces of death so his miraculous distribution of bread can continue (6:47–52).

Jesus Breaks Barriers to Table Fellowship (7:1–23)

A formidable obstacle blocked the way toward one bread and one world united in a covenant of peace. According to custom and tradition, Jewish people had to purify their hands from Gentile dust before meals. Food had to be pure and cooked by their own hands, not foreigners'. Also, they could not eat certain foods, especially pork, which were considered unclean. These biblically derived requirements made any real association and table fellowship with Gentiles practically impossible. Was there any authoritative word from Jesus to deal with this most difficult impediment? Actually, there was no specific word, since Jesus himself kept all these customs and rarely came into contact with Gentiles. However, he did give a principle on one occasion that could be a guide: "There is nothing outside a person that by going in can defile, but the things that come out are what defile." From this statement Mark drew a conclusion for his audience: "Thus he declared all foods clean" (7:23)

A Foreign Woman Opens Up a Whole New World (7:24–30)

An anonymous woman, representing the non-Jewish world, initiates a marvelous new direction in salvation history. Jesus is staying in mostly Gentile territory in southern Lebanon, but only privately. So when a Gentile woman asks for her daughter's cure, he responds, "Let the children be fed first." This is because the scriptures described the coming Messiah as being first for Israel, with the Gentiles joining them at the end of time (see, for example, Isaiah 2:1–4). This woman, however, will not take no for an answer. She persistently asks with deep faith to share this bread, even if only crumbs from the messianic banquet—the feeding that has just taken place. Jesus is deeply moved by her faith and replies in two ways: First, by curing her daughter from a distance, the only time in this Gospel. For the Gentile Gospel audience this is exciting; it means that Jesus heals them also across distance and time. Second, Jesus himself begins a second multiplication of bread that will answer the desire of the whole world that this woman represents.

A Deaf Man Hears Jesus' Voice (7:31-37)

The theme of universality with its joy and excitement continues for Mark's largely Gentile audience. In the same non-Jewish territory, Jesus heals a man who cannot hear or speak. The crowds remark, "He has done everything well." This is a wellness or peace refrain from the great universal creation theme in Genesis. There, at the end of each day, God saw that everything he had created was good. Like the healed man, the audience also can hear what they have never heard before, and speak as never before in God's new creation.

Jesus Feeds Four Thousand People (8:1–10)

Many details in this story show that it symbolizes a feeding of the whole non-Jewish world. For example, it takes place on Jesus' initiative in Gentile territory, and the people come "from a great distance." The numbers are indicative: *seven*, the number of fullness in regard to the original loaves and the baskets left over; *four*, the universal number of north, south, east, and west. Contrast this to the typically Jewish numbers of the first feeding which are *five*, representing the first five books of the Bible, and *twelve*, representing the *twelve* tribes of Israel. And most interesting is the phrase, *After giving thanks*, where the Greek root *eucharistia* is used instead of the more Jewish *blessing* in the first story.

The Pharisees' Yeast—A Contrast to
One Bread for One World (8:14-21)

A rude awakening and contrast comes on Jesus' return to Israel when Pharisees ask for a sign from heaven instead of the interior faith we have seen in the Greek woman. The sign requested was some great external and cosmic event such as thunder, lightning, or an earthquake. Jesus refuses. The only sign he promotes is the humble one of believing there can be a new food language for the world. Jesus warns his disciples not to fall into the same trap as their opponents: "Beware of the yeast of the Pharisees and the yeast of Herod." Like them, the disciples have trouble with Jesus' simple sign of bread taken and shared at his command. The key words are the *one loaf* they have in the boat. It should have been a reminder of Jesus' design to unite the world by sharing the same one bread. So Jesus challenges them and the Gospel audience to open their eyes and ears to this new meaning. They need to *remember* this whenever they eat together. Whenever they remember, they will experience Jesus' presence in a new bread destined to bring the world together in a covenant of peace.

Healing the Blind Man and the Gospel Transition Point (8:22–26)

We have just seen how the disciples were blind to the full meaning of the loaves. But Mark shows there is hope for them and disciples of any time. Jesus can open their eyes to understand who he is and what is the mysterious bread that he gives. This will take place in the two steps symbolized by the cure of the blind man. The first step will be the partial opening of Peter's eyes in the next scene; the second will be Jesus' coming instruction on the Son of Man and the way of the cross.

Peter's Partial Confession of Jesus as Messiah and the Teaching on the Son of Man (8:27–33)

The first gradual opening of eyes (from 8:24) takes place as Peter makes his confession of faith: "You are the Messiah." But Jesus sharply silences him and the others because it is insufficient. People can misunderstand him as a military Messiah at present or later returning from heaven to conquer their enemies. At this point, Mark presents the second stage of eye opening with the startling words: "Then he began to teach them that the Son of Man must undergo great suffering...be rejected...killed...and after three days rise again." Mark will have three such predictions (here, 9:30, and 10:32), each followed by an instruction on how to follow Jesus' way.

The title *Son of Man* again reminds the audience of the Book of Daniel, chapter seven. There, the title goes beyond that of the coming judge to represent the tiny people of God in their sufferings and humiliation. Yet they will be exalted and overcome the powerful rulers of the Greek Empire by reopening their closed Temple once more. This was celebrated by Jesus, and to this day in the feast of Chanukah in December. The strong word *must* shows a necessity in God's plan as found in the scriptures. This way of God is so difficult that Peter complains about it to Jesus. Jesus sharply replies, "Get behind me, Satan," for Peter is tempting him to abandon God's plan.

Then Jesus begins the first section of teachings on discipleship by saying to the Gospel audience: "If any want to become my followers, let them deny themselves, and take up their cross and follow me." He adds that if anyone is ashamed to follow this way, then the Son of Man in his return as judge will likewise be ashamed of that person. Here we note for the first time the coming of the Son of Man as future judge. It is likely that Mark expected this within the lifetime of the first Gospel audience, so he notes Jesus' words that some present will not die until they see that the kingdom of God has come with power.

The Transfiguration of Jesus and Coming Attractions for the Audience (9:2–8)

To confirm Jesus' teaching on his return as Son of Man and on the cross, Mark gives us a preview or "coming attractions" of that return. The high mountain recalls the mountain where Moses met God and his face was transfigured with divine light (Exod 34:29–35). Jesus will return like Elijah, whom God took up into heaven in a fiery chariot to await his command to return to earth in the new age (2 Kgs 2:11–12; Mal 4:5). The focal point of the vision is God's thunderous voice like that on Mount Sinai: "This is my son, my beloved, listen to him." At Jesus' baptism, God spoke directly to him and he faithfully obeyed. Now the disciples and Gospel audience are the ones whom the divine voice commands to really listen to the very difficult words of Jesus about taking up the cross and following him even at great personal risk. Here we will take excerpts of the Son of Man teachings of Jesus following each of his three predictions of suffering and death.

Faith in the Impossible: Healing of the Possessed Boy (9:14–29)

Mark could be called the Gospel of the Impossible. The way of the cross is so difficult that it takes extraordinary faith to follow it. In this story, the desperate case is a boy with frightful seizures that made him speechless and reduced him to a deathlike stupor. The boy's father had brought him to some disciples for a cure, but they were unable to help. The distraught father then introduced his son to Jesus with the words, "If you are able to do anything, have pity on us and help us." He imagined that Jesus would have powers superior to those of his disciples. However, in a striking manner, Jesus turns his words around: *"If you are able"*—placing the brunt on the faith of the recipient—"all things are possible for the one who believes."

The man humbly replies that he does not have that kind of faith and asks for it as a gift. This is a great relief for the audience. They also can be doubtful, wavering, and even argue with God. They identify with the disciples' question, "Why couldn't we cast it out?" The answer sounds simple—*prayer.* However, this does not just mean repeating a formula. It means total, intensive, persevering prayer that requires an inner struggle like that of the boy's father.

The Second Son of Man Prediction and Teachings (9:30—10:31)

The central theme of this second section on discipleship is that of the child, with stories of children told directly or indirectly. The connection to the Son of Man is very striking. That image was about little Israel confronting and overcoming the Greek Empire, prelude to that of the Romans. In Mark's time, the image becomes apropos for the surprising power of "little ones" to win over Rome or any other world empire. This is in line with the power of these little ones in a world of *shalom*.

Who Is the Greatest? (9:33–37)

Jesus' disciples were as competitive as we are today. Jesus' approach is not a negative, "don't argue or compete," but actually an encouragement to compete even more strongly for the "lowest" position of service: "Whoever wishes to be the first must be last and servant of all." Jesus places a little child in their midst as an object lesson. "Whoever welcomes one such child welcomes me." It is not a matter of *what* we do but *how* we do it. A welcome for a child, on the bottom power rung of society, is a welcome to Jesus and the God who sent him. The success of Tolkien's *The Lord of the Rings* may be due to the paradox that a little one, a hobbit, can overcome all the evil one's powers. This is because it is completely beyond the mind of evil forces that anyone would renounce or destroy a ring of power.

Jesus' View on Competition from Outsiders and Abuse of Little Ones (10:42–49)

No less a VIP than the apostle John tries to stop an outsider, a Jewish exorcist who was not a follower of Jesus. Jesus extends the example of welcome to an outsider who is like the "little one" or child above. Mark's Gospel warns against exclusivism. Again it is the quality of the reception that matters—even a cup of water to drink counts as given to the Messiah and merits a special reward. In contrast, the crime of those who abuse children or scandalize them is so great that no punishment would be enough. Likewise, extreme care must be taken to prevent this from happening (10:43–48). It is significant that Mark mentions hell, literally *gehenna*, only in this section, where it is found three times.

Peace and Love Begin at Home (10:1–31)

Mark prepares for a collection of household teachings with the phrase, "Have salt in yourselves and *be at peace with one another* (9:50). Salt was often used in establishing covenants (Lev 2:13). Any effort to have a Temple of Peace for the world must start with peace and affection at home. Instructions on marriage, children, and possessions follow. This will receive greater detail when we study Matthew. In regard to children, Mark's Gospel, with his focus on Jesus' feelings, has the most tender description of the gospels: "He took them up in his arms, laid his hand on them and blessed them" (10:16). This real affection is the only remedy for the abuse previously condemned. A blessing was a communication of divine energy, a sharing of all that is best.

The story of the rich young man is found in this collection because the extended household was the center of economy. Also, the matter of sharing possessions was a practical response to Jesus' mission to preach repentance in view of the kingdom. Perhaps contrasting with the children's blessing above, here is the story of a man who considered himself blessed by God in his many possessions. He had sincerely kept God's commandments since a youth and asked Jesus if there was anything else he could do. "Jesus, looking at him, loved him." This represents the loving invitation of grace going out to a gospel audience.

However, discipleship is not easy: "Go sell what you own, and give the money to the poor, and you will have treasure in heaven; then come follow me." To follow Jesus calls for a lifelong priority for the needs of the hungry and poor. This choice, then and now, is very difficult. "When the rich man heard this, he was shocked and went away grieving, for he had many possessions." Jesus follows the biblical teaching on land and property: It belongs to God, is lent for our use, and is meant to be equitably shared by all. The sadness and grieving of this man in facing this prospect was simply too much for him. He is anonymous because he represents many in the Gospel audience.

Since Jesus' teaching on money is so difficult, he repeats it three times, finally through a vivid and humorous image: "It is easier for a camel to go through the eye of a needle, than for someone who is rich to enter the kingdom of God." The apostles, like the rich man, were astounded in view of the common belief that rich people were blessed by God. They said to one another, "Who then can be saved?" Jesus replies that the ability to share generously is God's gift and very contrary to the human tendency toward selfishness: *"For mortals it is impossible, but for God all things are possible."*

From what follows, we learn that Jesus' focus is not just on giving up, but on finding unexpected additional personal wealth through sharing. Jesus said to Peter that the temporary loss of individual wealth would result in a new "commonwealth" in communities that truly share. This commonwealth, unlike earthly riches, cannot be taken away but endures into the next life. God's way is the reversal of ordinary human priorities: "But many who are first will be last and the last will become first."

The Third Prediction of Jesus' Death and Resurrection and Special Favors (10:32–52)

Jerusalem, the capital city, is now the immediate focus of the third prediction. As a prophet, Jesus must be ready to preach there and meet his most powerful opposition at the center of religious and political authority. Accordingly, there is an atmosphere of foreboding and fear as Jesus walks ahead of his disciples on the Jerusalem road. Jesus' predictions become more explicit and ominous. Yet James and John, leaders among the Twelve, were looking for special niches of power at Jesus' side in the capital city. Jesus warns them that they do not know what they are asking for. To be at Jesus' right hand or left hand (the audience will later hear) is the place of those crucified with Jesus on Calvary (15:27).

To be truly at his side, they would need to be *baptized* (plunged into) his death and share his *cup* of suffering. Jesus does not grant prizes in his kingdom. The story surprises us because we imagine Jesus' first followers with haloes around their heads and we tend to believe that competition and desire for power had no place among them. Mark believes in honesty and tells the story because he knows from experience that these realities of human weakness will plague the church at all times and need to be brought out in the open. "When the ten heard this, they began to be angry with James and John." The other ten disciples seem to have caught the same "capital fever" as they approach Jerusalem.

Mark was well aware of abusive Roman authority as he wrote Jesus' words, "Among the Gentiles, those whom they recognize as their rulers lord it over them." Yet the evangelist was even more sensitive to abusive church/community authority through Jesus' words addressed directly to the audience: *It is not so among you.* Jesus' followers are to be remarkable for loving service of others, not control over them. The supreme example is that of the Son of Man, who though coming as judge in power "came not to be served but to serve and to give his life as a ransom for many." The final words are adapted from the image of the Servant of the Lord in Isaiah 53 who offered his life to God as if a Temple sacrifice. This picture of himself as a living Temple links to the coming cleansing of the Temple and its replacement.

Healing of the Blind Bartimaeus and Its Symbolism (10:46–52)

Jericho, near the Dead Sea, marks the beginning of Jesus' final ascent to Jerusalem. This healing is very meaningful for an audience desiring in spirit to accompany Jesus to Jerusalem. They often become blind to the meaning of what will happen to Jesus in the capital and what it means to follow him there. The shouting, urgent prayer of Bartimaeus becomes that of anyone in the audience, "My teacher, let me see again." Once their sight is restored, like Bartimaeus they can follow him on the way.

Jesus' Triumphal Entry into Jerusalem as King of Peace (11:1–11)

The ancient kings of Israel often entered the capital in grandiose military style. The messianic entry of Jesus is a deliberately planned sharp contrast. He humbly enters the city seated on a donkey with a few disciples and followers. It resembled a clown act to teach his outlook on pretense and grandeur. As Mark's audience studied the scriptures, the inner Spirit of Jesus helped them understand the story in terms of Zechariah 9:9, "Your king will come to you, triumphant and victorious is he, humble and riding on a donkey." The text describes a Messiah of Peace who will destroy the chariots and weapons of war. (This text will be discussed in more detail in Luke and John. Mark tells the story so the listeners can replay it often in imagination and liturgical drama, singing with the crowds, "Hosanna! Blessed is the one who comes in the name of the Lord.")

The New Temple for All the World (11:12–25)

Mark relates this story in a neat literary frame with the fig tree lesson before and after it to highlight the power of Jesus' word about the new Temple. Time after time in teaching this episode, I have been asked "What about the poor fig tree?" Should ecologists be disturbed? Not if they have a sense of humor and see the fig tree in its proper place. The fig tree is a well-known symbol of the people of God. Jesus, like other prophets, used symbolic gestures. In this case, as a prophet, he is "hungry" and seeks "fruit" from his teaching. A curse in the scriptures indicates responsibility for rejecting God's voice in a prophet.

There is no question of wrongdoing on the part of those buying, selling, or changing money in the vast outside Temple court. Jews came to the feasts from all over the world and needed to change their money into local currency, which was required to purchase animals offered for sale in the same Temple area. This court was a large area, close to two football fields in size. Jesus' small symbolic cleansing focused on the priority of prayer in a new Temple designed for all the world's peoples. These Gentiles had been excluded by a formidable wall around part of the Temple area that warned them to go no farther under penalty of death.

The focus of the story is on Jesus' words, "My house shall be called a house of prayer for all the nations." Mark draws attention to the chief priests' and scribes' reaction to those words. We can hardly imagine their shock at the very thought that the sacred

Temple area (under their supervision!) would be a place where uncircumcised and pork-eating Gentiles would gather to pray with them. "When…they heard it, they kept looking for a way to kill him." In contrast, "The whole crowd was spellbound by his teaching." This could well describe the Gospel audience. As they listened to the story, they knew that the Temple had already been destroyed. Yet God had turned tragedy into triumph by giving them Jesus as a new spiritual Temple of worship, a house of peace and prayer for the whole world. In this form of worship, the buying and selling of animals, as symbolically stopped by Jesus, was no longer needed.

The reaction of Peter the next day on seeing the withered fig tree is very interesting. Like many readers, he was more interested in what happened to the fig tree. He missed the whole lesson on the powerful impact of Jesus' revolutionary announcement about creating a new world Temple where no one is excluded. It all sounds so impossible that Jesus continues with another humorous illustration—that of making a mountain move into the sea. Jesus explains the secret about how this can be done: "If you do not doubt, but believe that what you say will come to pass, it will be done for you." The recipe for success is having a faith so strong that you imagine the result even before you ask for it: "Whatever you ask for in prayer, believe that you have received it already and it will be yours."

The loss of the Temple was most serious, as a sign of the loss of God's presence and covenant. What will take its place when believers no longer have meeting places except in their homes? The answer is brought out in Jesus' answer as to what is the greatest commandment of all.

The Supreme Commandment in the New Temple (12:28–34)

The scribe's question, much disputed for thousands of years was "Which commandment is first of all?" Jesus replied in the words of the favorite Jewish prayer, the Shema ("Hear, O Israel," Deut 6:4–9) that was memorized and recited over and over during each day and especially at the hour of death. The words express a beautiful totality of devotion—mind, heart, and feelings—so there is really no place for what is more or less important. But Jesus continues on the same level, "You shall love your neighbor as yourself." The scribe realizes the radical conclusion that loving one's neighbor is far superior to all the Temple offerings, buildings, and religious rites. This is another Temple reference especially important for Mark's audience in the first centuries when they had no temples or church buildings but met in private homes. Their homes now became their Temple, where their love for one another was more important than any sacrifice. Mark previously had reported Jesus' saying, "Have peace with one another" (9:50).

Introduction to Jesus' Last Testament (12:38–40)

Jesus warns against pretentious religion teachers. The audience might smile at the familiar picture of religious leaders in fancy robes, prizing distinguished titles and sitting in specially reserved seats. Yet divisions based on rank corrode hopes for true peace in any community. The mention of widows is a connecting link and contrast to the next story of the poor widow that will introduce Jesus' last will and testament in the next chapter. The poor widow, unlike the scribes and rich people, did not just leave a donation in the Temple treasury, she "put in everything she had, all she had to live on." Thus, she is a living example of what Jesus will ask for in his last discourse: disciples willing to give everything, even life itself, for what they believe in. This is what really will move the Roman world.

We have previously discussed the impact of Jesus' last testament in chapter 13. It is preceded by the story of the poor widow and followed by that of the woman at Bethany. These two parallel one another and form an important literary frame around Jesus' words. Yet chapter 13 is so important for the image of Jesus as a Messiah of peace that it needs to be discussed in more detail.

The Temple's Destruction, Violent and Peaceful Messiahs, and Jesus' Return (13:1–37)

Jesus' last discourse and final testament informs his disciples what the future holds for them. By the time this Gospel was written, the Temple had already been destroyed in the recent past. This was a great shock both to Christians and Jews alike. It had been their religious center and place of worship as God's dwelling place. Some Christian prophets were teaching that the Temple's destruction was a divine sign heralding the imminent end of the world. During that time, Jesus would return in power to liberate them from their Roman oppressors and start a new age. Those prophets pointed to many signs to support their predictions. Jesus regards their teachings as false and dangerous.

The scene takes place on Mount Olivet, facing the Jerusalem Temple and a traditional place for God's coming judgment. Jesus predicts that the Temple will be destroyed. He warns his disciples about teachers who announce this, using the typical prophetic first person in Jesus' name, "I am he" (6). "When you hear of wars and rumors of wars, do not be alarmed" (7). This refers to false prophets who claimed that God's final battle against the forces of evil was about to begin. Jewish literature had predicted such a final conflict. It is interesting that government and military leaders through the centuries have always tried to make their soldiers believe they were fighting for both God and country in a great struggle against evil. Thus, soldiers could feel that even if they lost their lives they would become heroic and glorious martyrs. The false prophets also made predictions of natural phenomena such as earthquakes to bolster their claims.

From these false signs, Jesus turns to the true signs that will occur in believers' lives. Their future fate will be no different from that of Jesus—this will be the only real sign. Like Jesus, they will be handed over to councils, synagogues, and kings. This will not be a disaster but an opportunity for witness, a testimony *(martyrion)* to them. This will be the only way to win over others (like the way Jesus will win over a hardened centurion at his crucifixion). "And the good news [gospel] must first be proclaimed to all the nations" (10). This preaching to the world is another necessary prelude to Jesus' return. However, it will only come about through the suffering witness of disciples. In this way they will have an active part in bringing about Jesus' return. Consequently, believers need not fear the future, for their work is that of the Holy Spirit. This Spirit will speak through them even though the most shocking things happen, such as betrayal by family members and friends. Disciples can be confident in Jesus' words, "The one who endures to the end will be saved."

Therefore, the tragic and sacrilegious destruction of the Temple does not mean that God will swiftly intervene to destroy their enemies. Christians must not follow military or government leaders who proclaim this. Instead, Jesus advises flight: "[T]hose in Judea must flee to the mountains." *As Messiah of Peace and non-violence, Jesus does not support holy wars against "evildoers."* Believers should choose to flee rather than hope God will give them a victory over Rome despite overwhelming odds against them.

Again Jesus warns, three times in all, against false messiahs and false prophets who "produce signs and omens to lead astray if possible even the elect." Their teaching seduces many people because no one wants to be a loser, and surely God Almighty is on the winning side. It explains why Jesus and many prophets past and present receive such a limited popular reception. Prophets of peace and nonviolence rarely gain a majority support in their lifetimes. After their death, however, guilt often prompts people to name streets after them and declare holidays in their name.

As to the final return of the Son of Man, the fulfilled prediction regarding the Temple gives the audience additional confirmation that Jesus' further prediction of his return will also be accomplished. However, this return will not be local or connected with the Temple's tragic destruction. Instead, it will be a manifestation to the whole world. The sun, moon, and stars in the text stand for all creation. The Son of Man "will send his angels to gather his elect from the four winds." Thus, there will be no adverse judgment for any of the Gospel listeners who are not ashamed to stand up for what they believe (8:38).

All this points to the need for watchful waiting and prayer. Yet Jesus said, "About that day or hour no one knows" (13:32). This is a clear and definite answer to the disciples' question about the time of Jesus' return. Yet despite its clarity, hundreds of self-proclaimed prophets through the ages have deluded people into believing they have secret revelations about the exact time of the world's end and Jesus' return. Nevertheless, Christian faith does look forward to the future with hope combined with a present sense of responsibility. Since we have no knowledge or control over the future, Jesus repeatedly warns us to be *alert* and not *asleep* lest we miss once-and-for-all opportunities. This is illustrated in the concluding parable: "It is like a man going on a journey, when he leaves home and puts his servants in charge each with their own work" (34). Jesus is like that man on a journey, with each person having a charge. Disciples are asked to be faithful to the talent the Master has given them any time he asks for an accounting.

A Model in Action: How One Woman's Story Will Be Told Everywhere (14:1–9)

The heart of the Gospel, the passion narrative, now begins as the Jerusalem leaders seek to arrest Jesus secretly and execute him. Just as the poor widow's story introduced and exemplified Jesus' last testament, so also the Bethany woman introduces the story of Jesus' last days. She is purposely anonymous to give hope to all the anonymous persons among believers who wonder if their lives can be really worthwhile in creating a world of peace.

Women often performed part of the welcoming ritual of hospitality by anointing a guest's head with oil. But this lady's ointment was extravagant and lavish—she had worked hard for a year or more to earn the money to buy it. The breaking of the alabaster jar (like similar broken jars found in ancient cemeteries) symbolized the *pouring out* of her life. So she is like Jesus, for the same word describes his poured-out blood at the Last Supper (14:25). The fragrant perfumed ointment, *nard*, is found only in the biblical love poems of the Song of Solomon. It symbolizes the deep affection in her heart. Some disciples were angry about this and scolded the woman for her wastefulness: Would not a large donation to the poor be a better way to honor Jesus?

The above contrast is similar to the widow's story where the woman's gift of herself outweighed all the rich donations to the Temple treasury. Jesus replies by stressing the personal nature of the Bethany woman's gift: "Why do you trouble her? She has performed a good service for me. For you always have the poor with you...but you will not always have me." It is always possible and necessary to help the poor, but the total personal and affectionate gift of the woman is truly unique. She has appreciated the meaning of Jesus' coming death. Her anointing symbolizes that he will be the Messiah ("anointed one") through the offering of his life: "She has anointed my body beforehand for its burial." Parallel to the ending of the widow's story (12:43), Jesus concludes with a solemn Amen-I-say-to-you statement: "Wherever the good news is proclaimed in the whole world, what she has done will be told in remembrance of her." Following this woman's leadership, the personal devotion and service of seemingly unknown and anonymous people will make possible the spread of the gospel to the whole world. Only *whole* selfless actions such as this create a *whole* world of peace.

The Betrayal of Judas: A Model of Compliance and False Peace (14:10–11)

In contrast, Judas was surely among those who scolded the Bethany woman. At least the Gospel of John thought so (12:4). Over the centuries, Judas' character has become progressively blackened, yet we have little information about his inner motives. It is possible that he simply did his duty to the Roman puppet government (the chief priests) and denounced Jesus as a potential and therefore dangerous Messiah. For the audience, he represents those who play it safe and are not willing to take the risks necessary to follow Jesus. Security, safety, and compliance were the slogans of the Pax Romana enforced by the Roman military. This is the opposite of true peace, which involves nonconformity, daring, and risk.

Jesus' Last Supper and Covenant Passover Meal with His Disciples (14:12–21)

"On the first day of the Unleavened Bread when the Passover lamb is sacrificed," begins the narrative. Mark explains the meaning of Jesus' action through its strong parallel to the Passover ritual. The Passover meal was celebrated according to God's precise instructions in Exodus 12. This gave the ritual its power. In parallel, Jesus gives exact orders about the planning of this meal. There are unusual circumstances, such as the meeting of a man carrying a water jar who brings them to a furnished banquet hall. This shows that the divine plan is beneath what is happening on the surface. The meal will indeed be *The Lord's Supper*, arranged at his command and therefore having his power.

Evening sundown signaled the time for the Passover meal to begin when Jesus arrived with his disciples. Unfortunately, art masterpieces showing only Jesus and twelve male disciples have given us a wrong image: Women had to be present according to the Passover regulations of Exodus 12. As they were eating, Jesus made the shocking announcement that one of his table companions would betray him. He assures them that this is not just a horrible accident but that God's plan will work despite it and even through it.

The loaves' multiplication has already prepared for the Last Supper: The disciples are to remember Jesus when they break bread (8:18). Now the evangelist presents the ritual way to do this as it was planned and executed by Jesus. The loaves' multiplication illustrated the nourishing quality of bread given by Jesus as good shepherd. But there is also another central bread meaning, that of covenant or contract. Meals in ancient times often sealed contracts and agreements between people. The English language has a relic of this in the word *companion*, from the Latin roots *cum* (with) and *panis* (bread).

Also, bread has a strong identification motif: "We are what we eat." This motif is especially strong when the host furnishes the bread and serves it by hand after breaking it. Thus the command, "Take, this is my body," is a challenge and invitation to be truly identified with Jesus as a disciple. The shared cup strengthens this and brings out the covenant aspect. For example, at a Jewish wedding, even to this day, bride and bridegroom drink from the same cup to signify their covenant with one another. Mark writes, "So all of them drank from it."

The words "This is my blood" recall Moses' words when he sealed a covenant between God and his people on Mount Sinai. Moses took sacrificial blood and sprinkled it on the people, saying, "See the blood of the covenant that the LORD has made with you" (Exod 24:8). Jesus added that his blood (in view of his death) is poured out for many. The symbolism of wine for blood is largely lost by a modern audience. The wine color is only a minor element. The Semitic expression for wine, usually red, was "the blood of the grape." This originates in the wine-making process: People trampled upon the grapes until they "died" and gave out their "blood." Finally, Jesus said, "Truly I tell you, I will never again drink of the fruit of the vine until the day when I drink it new in the kingdom of God." This final emphatic amen statement of Jesus shows his determination to go ahead and his confidence that he will again return after death to eat and drink with them.

The Last Supper was a covenant of peace both with God and with his disciples. With God, because he was going ahead with his vocation to bring the good news of repentance to the capital even at the risk of death. These are the elements of sacrifice. With his disciples, because they were pledging to join him in this by sharing his bread and drinking his cup.

Peter Abandons the Last Supper Covenant but Is Forgiven (14:26–31; 66–72)

Any audience past or present finds it hard to accept Jesus' words, "You will all become deserters." The story shows that, despite failures to keep their Last Supper covenant of peace, God will still be faithful, forgive, and continue to work through them. Jesus assures the disciples that even if God allows the good shepherd to be struck down and the sheep scattered, he will return to go before them in Galilee once more. Peter will not believe this and protests that he will not be like the others. So Jesus has to repeat his prediction and single him out. After Jesus' arrest, Peter chose the false peace of security and compliance like Judas. However, unlike Judas he remembered Jesus' words and wept bitterly. His conversion will be marked in the last verses of the Gospel where the angels tell the women to "go tell Peter" (16:7).

Jesus' Temptation, Decision, and Arrest: An Audience Model (14:23–51)

This is the agonizing decision time of the passion narrative. It was the last chance for Jesus, under cover of night, to return to Galilee where he had strong support. Yet he knew that God had called him to preach in Jerusalem, the capital, like Jeremiah and other prophets. Jesus' prayer is a long struggle to make the right decision. More than other gospels, Mark presents this with all the realities of human weakness seeking divine strength. Jesus falls prostrate on the ground and prays, "Abba, Father, for you all things are possible; remove this cup from me; yet not what I want, but what you want."

Abba, Aramaic for "Father," is the exact word used by Jesus. It is still used in Israel and parts of Syria by children addressing their fathers. The accent is on devotion to God as a faithful child: "Not what I want, but what you want." Jesus repeats these words over and over to gain strength to face his coming arrest. Three times Jesus returns to his disciples to encourage them to pray, but finds them asleep. This note is for an audience who may also face arrest or suffering if they are faithful to their beliefs. They will fail or desert Jesus like Peter and the Twelve unless they pray like Jesus did for divine strength. Finally, Jesus feels within him that he has received that strength. He then departs to give himself up voluntarily to Judas and the crowd coming to arrest him.

The armed crowd, led through the dark night by Judas, quickly arrests Jesus after Judas' prearranged treacherous identification kiss. After a brief armed resistance by a disciple, Jesus states that he is not a revolutionary relying on force, power, and secrecy. If they arrest him, it is not a sign of weakness but of his desire to do what God asks of him. The same would be true of any of the audience. Mark then records the sad words, "All of them deserted him and fled." Jesus had expected and even predicted this, yet this did not lessen the pain of that moment.

Jesus' Trial and Confession Before the Ruling Council (14:53–65)

Mark's principal concern is to contrast, for audience reflection, between Jesus' heroic confession and Peter's gradual withdrawal and denial. When questioned by authority, Jesus bravely confesses who he is and what he stands for: "the Messiah, Son of the Blessed One." This is the only open confession Jesus makes in this Gospel, though it will lead to his death. The judges of Jesus were a group of priests, scribes, and elders. They constituted the puppet religious and political senate, at the head of which was the high priest who was appointed by the Roman governor. The judges needed false witnesses: "Some said they had heard him say, 'I will destroy this Temple that is made with hands and in three days I will build another, not made with hands.'" Jesus had never said these words. Yet they were strangely true for the Gospel audience who understood that Jesus' death would make possible a new universal Temple of God. This was also foreshadowed in the Temple cleansing story.

In response to his judges, Jesus responded that he would return as the Son of Man and judge to vindicate the truth of his confession to be Messiah and Son of God. The high priest then ritually tore his garments as a sign of blasphemy against God. Jesus' confession may have been more evident to the audience than to those actually present at Jesus' trial. Whatever the nature of this blasphemy, Jesus' claim to be Messiah constituted a charge that could serve as a basis for trial before the Roman governor who had jurisdiction over such serious matters. Any claim to be a king was a threat to Rome and against the decrees of Caesar. (An example may be found in Acts 17:7.)

Jesus Before Pilate: Messiah of Peace or War? (15:1–15)

The ruling council brings Jesus to Pilate, the Roman governor, for a trial and sentence. There is no question about the nature of this charge, for Pilate asks Jesus, "Are you the king of the Jews?" In other words, a messiah or anointed one, the greatest threat to Roman power. The same title on the cross provides the reason for Jesus' execution. All in all, the title occurs six times in this chapter. Rome alone is responsible for the sentencing and execution of Jesus. Expressions like "the Jews killed Jesus" are a horrible travesty of the truth that has contributed to untold suffering for millions of innocent people through the centuries. Jesus is silent and will not admit the charges. The words "You say so" mean that Jesus has not been a messiah in Pilate's military sense.

Pilate offers the crowd the release of a prisoner of choice at Passover time. Barabbas is a revolutionary leader who was guilty of murder during a revolt. As such, he awaited execution in prison. Yet the small crowd assembled by the rulers asks for his release rather than that of Jesus. The choice is one for the audience as well. What type of Messiah do they want—Jesus, a nonviolent Messiah of Peace, or Barabbas a leader of violence and power? Barabbas in Aramaic means "son of the father," so the contrast to Jesus is quite evident. The crowd actually chooses someone like themselves, for they keep shouting for Jesus' crucifixion—becoming murderers like Barabbas. Finally, "he [Pilate] handed him over to be crucified." This handing over is to the Roman soldiers in the next verse under the command of a Roman centurion (15:15).

The Roman Soldiers Mock Jesus (15:16–20)

The soldiers played a familiar game. This involved dressing up and crowning someone as emperor and making him the object of all kinds of mockery, jokes, and cruel, rough, even brutal treatment. Excavated parts of the original stone pavement have uncovered marks on stones for these games. For the audience, some of whom had been soldiers, the contrast is striking: Those who bend their knees in mockery will someday actually worship a disgraced, crucified Messiah. God's power of turning humiliation and disgrace into triumph is a great joyful surprise to an audience of any time. "King of the Jews" is the title of a lowly Messiah of Peace.

The Crucifixion of Jesus and Its Meaning (15:21–32)

This account does not furnish the details and descriptions of a modern newspaper. The whole focus is on the meaning of Jesus' death in terms of God's plan in the scriptures. "They compelled a passerby…to carry the cross." Mark notes this because Simon, an African from the Roman province of Cyrene, is the first person, like Jesus, to carry the cross. He did so unwillingly, yet with a tremendous impact on his own life and the lives of others. He became the father of Alexander and Rufus, converted Christians known to Mark's audience. The message is forceful: God asks no one to carry the cross with a smile; patient endurance will have its own unexpected fruit in time and deeply affect others. Golgotha (which means "place of the skull") was a familiar place by the road to Jerusalem for frequent public executions and horrible sufferings. "They offered him wine mixed with myrrh but he did not take it." A drugged wine would have eased his pain, but Jesus chose to be as alert as possible to the end.

"And they crucified him and divided his garments among them, casting lots." The details of crucifixion are too horrible for description. Mark selects those illustrating that Jesus' death is not just a frightful tragedy and accident but that God's mysterious transforming plan is at work. The main scripture selected is Psalm 22 on the theme of the suffering and triumph of a just servant of God. In verse 18 of this psalm we find a mention of dividing garments and casting lots. In other words, soldiers appear to do this just to make their customary extra profit. However, beneath their actions the divine plan is at work. "And with him they crucified two bandits, one on his right, one on his left." These "bandits" were revolutionaries who resorted to violent theft to finance their efforts. To all appearances, Jesus is just another one of them.

While on the cross, three different groups contribute to a last temptation of Christ to prove his cause by power. First of all, the passersby shake their heads in mocking disbelief. Once again the Temple theme recurs, for Jesus will accomplish their taunting remarks in God's mysterious ways: "Aha, you who would destroy the temple and build it in three days, save yourself and us." *It is precisely through the cross that the new world Temple will be built by God.* What could be more ludicrous than a helpless Messiah! The chief priests and scribes take up the same theme, pretending they would be ready to believe if Jesus came down from the cross. The third group is the two others at Jesus' right and left hand.

Jesus' Death, the Opening of the Temple Veil, and the Roman Centurion's Conversion (15:33–39)

The darkness over the whole land symbolizes the cosmic significance of Jesus' death, a foreshadowing of his future return as Son of Man (13:24). The evangelist focuses on Jesus' last words in his own Aramaic language, translated, "My God, my God *[Eli, Eli]*, why have you forsaken me?" (from Psalm 22:1). The dark atmosphere of apparently complete abandonment, even by God, is meant for the audience so they can have hope during similar feelings, especially under persecution. The same Psalm 22 has this hope in the second part of its prayer. Some bystanders misunderstood Jesus' words and thought he was calling on Elijah. For the audience, Elijah was the popular patron of a happy death, since God delivered him from death in a fiery chariot (1 Kgs 2:11). Elijah was expected to return to help the just in their last hour (Mal 4:5). But no Elijah comes to help Jesus and even this hope turns into derision. Nor will Elijah suddenly intervene for the audience if they face loneliness and abandonment like Jesus.

"Then Jesus gave a loud cry and breathed his last." Such a loud strong cry would hardly be expected from someone completely debilitated and ready to die after three hours on the cross. It is a supreme sign of victory despite every appearance of utter failure. The vibrating power of that cry opens up the Temple veil and access to divine forgiveness for all. This had been previously an exclusive privilege of the Jewish people. The high priest negotiated this once a year on the feast of Yom Kippur by entering the Holy of Holies to sprinkle sacrificial blood on the sacred Ark of the Covenant to obtain forgiveness of sin for the people of Israel (Lev 16). But now forgiveness would be extended to the least likely prospect.

"Now when the centurion, who stood facing him, saw that in this way he breathed his last," the narrative continues. This Roman centurion was a professional executioner. He had been a hardened and insensitive man, skilled in frequently supervising the most cruel, torturous death ever devised by the human race. The manner of Jesus' death so impressed the centurion that he made the climactic confession of faith in the Gospel: "Truly this man was God's son." Yes, Jesus' death was worthwhile and made a difference by winning over this Roman, a first fruit and example of many future believers. It tells the audience that each person's life can make a real difference and impact on the world if their life stands behind what they believe in. They become the co-builders of Jesus' world Temple of Peace.

More surprises are ahead for the audience: "There were also women looking on from a distance. Among them were Mary Magdalene and others who had followed him from Galilee." Their actual names occur three times: here, 15:47, and 16:1. This is important because they are the essential witnesses of Jesus' actual death, place of burial, and resurrection. We noted Jesus' first words to his disciples in Galilee: "Follow me and I will make you fish for people" (1:17). Who actually *did* this? The stalwart Twelve had all abandoned him at his arrest. The only ones to follow him all the way from Galilee to the cross were these faithful women. Although the Gospel has the atmosphere of a male-dominated world, God does not act that way and turns human expectations upside down. Dedicated women made possible the fishing for people that Jesus promised. Women in the audience can identify with the *many women* that Mark notes in 15:41. These are the first *fisherwomen* who continued Jesus' work.

The Burial of Jesus (15:42–47)

Another effect of Jesus' death was to inspire still others to come out and take a stand. Joseph of Arimathea is one of these, since he risked his life by claiming Jesus' body. (This would make him suspect to Roman authority as a friend of a revolutionary.) Mark does not call him a disciple but a faithful Jew looking for God's kingdom. Thus we find both a Gentile Roman and a Jew together at Jesus' death. Pilate takes care to verify the certainty of Jesus' death. The details of wrapping the corpse and its burial also confirm this reality. "Then Joseph rolled a stone against the door of the tomb." This symbolizes the seal of death with all its irreversible power.

Jesus' Resurrection and Continued Presence as Shepherd (16:1–8)

"When the Sabbath was over, Mary Magdalene, and Mary the mother of James, and Salome bought spices, so that they might go and anoint him." On the first Easter Sunday, there was no press corps or television crew to cover the news. The faithful women alone come to the tomb to anoint his dead body as a last loving service. They kept talking to one another about the big problem ahead: "Who will roll away the stone for us from the entrance of the tomb?" But then, when they looked up they were utterly amazed when they "saw that the stone, which was large, had already been moved back." This is a special sign of divine intervention.

"And as they entered the tomb, they saw a young man, dressed in a white robe, sitting on the right side; and they were alarmed." The youth told them, "You are looking for Jesus of Nazareth, who was crucified. He has been raised; he is not here." Then the youth, seated in the place of authority on the right side of the tomb as a teacher gives them a final commission: "Go tell his disciples and Peter that he is going ahead of you into Galilee; there you will see him, just as he told you." Following this, we have what at first seems to be an abrupt ending to the Gospel:

"They [the women] went out and fled from the tomb, for terror and amazement had seized them; and they said nothing to anyone, for they were afraid."

This puzzling, incomplete ending has always been troublesome for almost two thousand years. Everyone likes to have a complete, happy, triumphant end to a story of a hero. To remedy this, some ancient copyists added a variety of endings to the Gospel, with many details taken from other gospels. (See the New Testament text notations.) Thousands of scholars have also struggled to interpret Mark's ending in a more favorable light.

However, why not just accept that Mark wanted the ending incomplete and that it needs to be completed by the audience? They have the assurance that Jesus will go before them as a good shepherd so they can begin again his ministry in Galilee and await his Second Coming: "There you will see him as he told you."

Summary Points for Praxis, Teaching, and Ministry

- Jesus announced his purpose to create a new Temple of Peace with the words that his house shall be called one of prayer for all the nations. This would break down the wall in the Temple court forbidding Gentiles further access. Followers of Jesus at any time are members of this new Temple with its goal to reach out to as many people as possible, especially those who feel excluded by race or other limitations.

- Jesus' baptism and mission of preaching repentance by words and lifestyle call is a model for believers. It involved risk in opposing those who did not wish to see the changes that this entailed. Jesus' words were so effective because he faced even death in the stands that he took in face of civil and religious authorities. The way of the cross is the only path for followers of Jesus.

- Mark is sometimes called the Gospel of the Impossible. Jesus tells the father of the boy suffering from convulsions:

"If you are able!—all things can be done for the one who believes" (9:23).

- The passion account presents Jesus as a Messiah of Peace and nonviolence. At his death, the veil of the Temple, signifying exclusive access to forgiveness, is symbolically shattered, bringing forgiveness even to a hardened centurion executioner. Thus the audience can hope that their faithful suffering can affect others in the same way. The resurrection story invites them to follow Jesus as good shepherd into Galilee, where he will again be with them in this mission.

- Mark is a do-it-yourself Gospel. Jesus was a healer of the whole person. His disciples also went out and "anointed with oil many who were sick and cured them" (6:13). The sacrament for the sick is not meant to be hoarded for special occasions, but applied as often as possible. While this is usually reserved for bishops and priests, any believer can be a minister of healing to others through prayer, blessing, healing touch, oils, or medicines.

$$3$$

THE GOSPEL OF MATTHEW: PEACEMAKING IN A DIVIDED COMMUNITY

*"Blessed are the peacemakers for they shall be
called children of God" (5:9)*

Only Matthew has the title *peacemakers*, along with their special privilege of being called children of God. It will be a special focus in this Gospel. But first we should summarize the situation for which this Gospel was written.

The Situation and Problems of Matthew's Community

Mark was the first written Greek Gospel. Matthew wrote his Gospel in the late first century, after Mark. However, Matthew incorporates considerable earlier Palestinian material from his sources. Mark had previously written during severe Roman persecution, after the destruction of Jerusalem in AD 70 during the Jewish War with Rome. For Mark's audience, time was short as they awaited Jesus' return even within their own lifetime. Jesus told them that their best witness was the willingness to suffer and even give one's life if necessary for their beliefs. However, Matthew's Gospel was written some decades afterward, with less anxiety over persecution, which was more from fellow Jews than from Gentiles. Matthew's emphasis is more on Jesus' authoritative words as a guide to good works in everyday life. This *present* focus is due to a different time perspective and the situation of Matthew's audience.

Affluent Members of Matthew's Community

The prime reason for a focus on good works is that many of Matthew's audience have settled down in the world and imitated secular values. There were rich households of believers along with an opposite extreme of very poor people. This atmosphere of affluence and its contrasts is reflected in the Gospel itself. Matthew is sometimes called the Golden Gospel because of its many descriptions of money, business, and wealth. The author describes many converts as upper-class scribes when Jesus spoke of tax collectors coming to John the Baptist in repentance (21:32). Writing itself was a profession in those days, and the scribe was trained in law, contracts, taxes, real estate, business, government, and diplomacy. Scribes were also the religious and secular (both went together) teachers as well. Many held important government positions. In the gospels, along with the chief priests, they were the leaders of the people. The training and education of a scribe furnished the gateway to success and wealth in the ancient world.

Matthew as a gospel writer was certainly a scribe and perhaps at times a tax collector before his conversion. He may have humorously changed the name of Levi (as in Mark and Luke), the tax collector called by Jesus, to Matthew because scribe was his profession also (9:9). On the list of apostles, he names himself "Matthew the tax collector" (10:3). Like Levi in the original story, he had many rich friends with whom he shared the good news of his conversion. Only this Gospel has a scribe asking Jesus if he can be a follower: "A scribe approached him [Jesus] and said, "Teacher, I will follow you wherever you go" (8:19). Jesus warned him not to expect the comfort and security that usually went with his profession: "Foxes have holes, and the birds of the air have nests; but the Son of Man has nowhere to lay his head." Matthew surely thought of himself in the concluding parable of chapter 13: "Every *scribe* who has been trained for the kingdom of heaven is like the master of a household who brings out of his treasure what is new and what is old" (13:52).

In regard to affluence, Matthew's Gospel is quite distinct from Luke. For example, Jesus is not born in humble circumstances and visited by poor shepherds. Instead, the Magi visit him in a *house* and share their wealth by bringing expensive gifts of gold, frankincense, and myrrh (2:1). Matching this rich atmosphere is the story of Jesus' burial. A rich man provides it. He places Jesus in his own new tomb, which he has designed and built perhaps over many years, for it is carved out of rock (27:57–60). A Gospel hero is a woman in a wealthy home who gives all she has saved for an expensive anointing perfume and pours it on Jesus' head. In return, Jesus tells her that the story of what she has done will be told all over the world (26:13). In the Sermon on the Mount, Jesus emphasizes inner detachment from riches: "Blessed are the poor *in spirit*" (5:3). However, in Luke's corresponding sermon, Jesus simply says, "Blessed are you poor" (6:20).

Other Gospel details lend support to calling Matthew the Golden Gospel. In fact it is the only Gospel that mentions gold. Matthew does this five times beginning with the regal gift of the Magi. There is a touch of humor in the contrast between Jesus' instruction to the apostles in Mark, Luke, and Matthew. In the first two, they are to take no money or purse or copper coins for their preaching tour (Mark 6:8; Luke 9:3). However, in Matthew they must not have gold, silver, or copper coins in their belts (10:9). This Gospel actually has more about the different types of money than any other gospel. Above all it has more descriptions of typical homes of more affluent people. This was the extended patriarchal household that we will now describe.

The Patriarchal Household in Matthew

The predominant economic unit in the Greek and Roman world was the extended household. The father and household manager was the *oikodespotēs*. The etymology of the word, from *oikos*, house, and *despotēs*, owner, lord, or manager already has sent its vibrations through the centuries into the dictionary where a *despot* means a tyrannical ruler. Here we will refer to the *oikodespotēs* as the "householder" or "household manager." This household was an extended residence consisting of the household master as well as father, the wife and children, and frequently relatives, workers, and slaves.

In the Roman world the translation of *oikodespotēs* was *paterfamilias*, a word that has even lingered in modern dictionaries as "the male head of a household" or "the father of a family." The early Latin version of Matthew carried *paterfamilias* as the usual translation of *oikodespotēs* Literally, the word meant "father of a family." Wherever Roman authority and power was established in the world, it soon became a familiar word. However, *paterfamilias* was much more than a title. In Roman law it was a juridic entity for the person who held the *patria potestas* or patriarchal power. This was an exclusive title of power over wives, children, slaves, and possessions. No other family member could enter into a transaction solely on their own. However, Romans sometimes permitted local regions to keep their own traditional laws.

The Householder and Household Structure in Hellenistic Judaism

The primary tradition of household authority even in the earlier Greek world was described by Aristotle. He considered the household as the primary unit of the city or state. Within the household he defines four areas: 1) husband and wife, 2) father over children, 3) master over slaves, 4) household management, supervision of workers and business. In each of these areas, there is hierarchal control: The husband rules over the wife; the father over the children; the master over the slaves; and the father as manager of the household and business matters.

The Book of Sirach (Ecclesiasticus) was written by a Jerusalem Judean in the second century BC. The author tries to win admiration for the Hebrew tradition of Wisdom and Law to encourage readers influenced and tempted by Hellenistic culture and learning. Within his book we find regulations and advice about the basic Jewish-Hellenistic household structure of husbands-wives, father-children, and master-slaves. For example, in regard to wives, the husband should not lightly divorce his spouse but at the same time not continue to entrust himself to her if he cannot love her (7:26). Sirach considers a quiet wife as a virtuous one: "A silent wife is a gift from the Lord; and nothing is so precious as her self-discipline" (26:14). Because of her status under control of the household head, her choices for marriage become limited by her father's will. While children were abused and controlled by physical means, women often suffered more from male verbal abuse and attitudes.

As to children, the author writes, "Do you have children? Discipline them and make them obedient from their youth. Do you have daughters? Be concerned for their chastity, and do not show yourself too indulgent with them. Give a daughter in marriage and you complete a great task; but give her to a sensible man" (7:23–25). Behind the word *discipline* there was often the cruel reality of harsh physical punishment. In a later passage we have the following: "He who loves his son will whip him often so that he may rejoice in the way he turns out" (30:1).

Philo was a Jewish scholar who lived in Alexandria, Egypt, about the time of 30 BC to AD 40. He represents the best source for Hellenistic Judaism in the period closest to Jesus' lifetime. Philo discusses household structure and duties in two of his books. In his study of the Ten Commandments, he includes the whole household under the commandment, "Honor your father and mother." For Philo this involves the relationship of old to young, rulers to subjects, and masters to slaves. The "superior class" consists of parents, elders, benefactors, and masters. The "lower class" includes children, young people, receivers of benefits, subjects, and slaves. In another book, he contrasts the values of the good and wicked. The latter despise "the best things of the world." These include honor to princes, the care of a wife, raising children, a proper relationship with slaves, and house management.

Josephus (from his Roman name, Flavius Josephus) was a Jewish commander in Galilee captured by the Romans early in their war with the Jews around the year AD 66. After the war he devoted himself to writing the history of the war and a history of his own people. Toward the end of his life around the year 100, he wrote a treatise, *Against Apion*. Book two of this work is a defense of the laws and customs of the Jews in answer to attacks on their character and history by Gentile philosophers and writers. In writing about marriage and children, his concern is to impress his readers with the strictness of Jewish ethics.

In this book, Josephus uses the title *despotēs* when writing about living under the law as under a father or master (2, 18). While defending Jewish laws of marriage, he presents a picture of well-regulated subordination of wives under their husbands (2, 25). He emphasizes wives' obedience and states that husbands have a God-given authority over them. He supports this by a quotation from scripture, "A woman is inferior to her husband in all things." However, this is nowhere to be found in the Hebrew scriptures. Regarding children, he writes that they are brought up in learning and practice of the laws. Parents are to be honored in the first place after God. Ungrateful sons are liable to the death penalty. Young men should respect elders because "God is the eldest of all beings" (2, 28).

The Christian "House of Peace"

Because of the above background, the house, *oikos* or *oikia*, is a favorite word in this Gospel, occurring about thirty-eight times. Matthew is concerned to present the image of a household of peace, typical of an ideal family of Jesus' disciples. When a household or home first received the messengers of good news, they heard the customary greeting of peace. But this was not an ordinary "peace." It was a greeting from God that carried his presence, energy, and peace. So Jesus tells his apostles, "As you enter the house, greet it. If the house is worthy, let your *peace* come upon it; but if it is not worthy, let your peace return to you" (10:12). So throughout the Gospel, the evangelist will provide model images of a "house of peace" that we will point out as we come to them.

The House of the Child Jesus and the Magi's Visit

The gospel childhood stories are largely what is called *midrash*. This Hebrew term means a literary form that weaves together biblical texts and traditions to discover the meaning of events in God's plan. Jesus' birth and childhood will foreshadow his whole career, especially the triumphant ending of his life despite rejection and apparent failure. Here the mysterious visit of the Wise Men from the East foreshadows the Gospel ending and Jesus' commission to bring the Gospel to all nations (28:16–20).

The Magi follow a star, perhaps a reference to Numbers 24:19, "A star shall come out of Jacob." The kings take a long journey of faith to reach King Herod of Israel. Then the paradox is striking: Herod, despite his deceit and evil intentions, actually directs the Magi to Bethlehem! (Note the Matthaean theme that God even turns evil into good.) On finding the child's home, "the wise men were overwhelmed with joy." This is the messianic joy the audience should experience knowing that God lavishes his gifts even on strangers and outsiders. The kings offer him appropriate gifts for a royal child—gold, frankincense, and myrrh. These gifts symbolize the joyful tribute of the whole world. This is because Psalm 72:10–15 uses similar words to describe the gifts that the kings of the world bring to Israel's king.

The text notes that "they entered the *house*" where the child, Mary, and Joseph were. This signifies the typical house of the believer where one can come and pay homage or worship, mentioned three times in 2:2, 8, 11. It is a perfect or complete house (thus a house of peace), for strangers and foreigners can join together with Mary and Joseph. In opening and sharing their regal gifts, their very best, the Magi make the house a place where such total sharing takes place. The strangers foreshadow the cross, for they worship "the king of the Jews." This is a title only found elsewhere in the passion account, where even the foreign Roman centurion and others worship Jesus at the foot of the cross bearing the title, "King of the Jews

The Sermon on the Mount

Matthew's Gospel centers about five neatly defined discourses: 1) The Sermon of the Mount, (5—7); 2) The Apostolic Instruction (10:1—11:1); 3) The Parables (13:1–53); 4) Church Discipline (18:1—19:1); 5) The Eschatological Discourse (24:1—26:1). While Mark stressed Jesus' actions for imitation, Matthew focuses more on Jesus' words and teachings that mediate his power and continued presence in the community/house/church. We place house and church side by side because the house was the place where the church (or assembly) actually met, since there were no specific church buildings until centuries later.

The most important of the five great discourses is the Sermon on the Mount, which is Matthew's compendium of Jesus' teaching. The collection goes far beyond anything in its original setting. Actually, it includes things said on other occasions in the other gospels. Not only that, the collection goes beyond Jesus' earthly life and presupposes his death, resurrection, and presence in his church. The atmosphere of the sermon is not legalistic or restrictive. It presupposes "amazing grace" and the resulting "costs of discipleship." The poetic form of Jesus' sayings made them easy to memorize and hand down for decades before they were put into written form for reference. The idea was not to simply remember facts but to be continually renewed and energized. People took the words to heart. They were addressed to a live audience by a living, risen Jesus.

The Beatitudes, Introductory Charter for a House of Peace (5:1–11)

Peace connotes wholeness, so Matthew stresses the inner nature of Jesus' teaching to complete the outward written covenant. "When Jesus saw the crowds, he went up the mountain." This is Matthew's favorite mountain theme. In the background is the fiery Mount Sinai, where God gave his commandments to his people through Moses. Here Jesus is enthroned (sits down) with divine authority like a new Moses to give his own teachings to his people. The Beatitudes are the keynote introduction providing a new interior basis for a meaningful life in contrast to the exterior things most people find so important.

"Blessed are the poor in spirit, for theirs is the kingdom of heaven." The Beatitudes get their name from the opening word *beatus*, the Latin word for "blessed" or "happy." Most people connect happiness with the "luck" to obtain exterior things such as money, power, recognition, sex, and so on. Jesus' teaching focuses within. The *poor in spirit* is a biblical reference to those who need God and not money to fill their desires. Thus, they have everything they need and the kingdom of heaven is theirs.

Those that mourn are those who feel sorry not for themselves but for others. With real compassion they sympathize with the sufferings of other people. "They shall be comforted." This and other parallels are in the passive voice in the typical Hebrew way of avoiding direct mention of God. Thus we would say, "God will comfort them." The Beatitudes have a strong future orientation. A present path of selflessness makes possible a future permanent joy. "Blessed are the meek." The meek are those who renounce violence and control over others—the very opposite of peace. In return, God gives them the whole earth as a gift. "Inheriting the earth" is symbolic of God's gifts since he had promised the land to his people. Those who "hunger and thirst for righteousness" are people whose real inner desire or "hunger" is for God's justice for everyone, though this means that at times they will choose to have less so that others will have enough. God will fill their desires and hunger. *The merciful* are those like God, whose great name is the "Merciful One." Being like God, they receive this mercy themselves in the fullest measure.

The pure of heart: In the Bible, the heart is the source of intention and desire. Matthew will emphasize this throughout his Gospel. Where the heart is simple, uncluttered, and pure, people will live in peace and be able to really see God with perfect eyesight. *The peacemakers:* Shalom sums up every blessing from God. These people bring into action the previous Beatitudes of peace. *Children of God* is often in the sense of imitation—someone who is like a parent, in this case, God. In the Bible, peace is not just a quality or attribute of God: "The LORD is peace" (Judg 6:24). "Those who are persecuted" can "rejoice and be glad." This is the surprising and "ridiculous" response of those who become grace-filled and like the Merciful One. It is rejoicing not from a love of suffering itself (nowhere praised in scripture) but rooted in being a bearer of God's message that has brought sufferings on many prophets.

The images of salt and light (5:13–14) conclude the Beatitudes. Jesus' teachings are meant to serve everyone. True disciples provide a flavor to the whole earth and a spark/light to the world. Their salt is not just to sprinkle on themselves but to give to others. "Let your light shine before others." This is not their light but God's. If genuine, it will be recognized by others and draw them to their Creator. Here we find another Matthaean theme that outsiders will be our judges as they observe and see what we do. This will be summed up in the final judgment scene (25:31–46). With Matthew's house of peace theme, the light within illuminates the whole house: "It gives light to all the house." It is like a bright city at night upon a hill: A city built on a hill cannot be hidden. This image is related to Jesus' first house in Bethlehem. The Magi followed the bright star until it came and stopped over the house and illuminated it. At this they were overwhelmed with joy.

Fulfillment and Perfection of the Torah, Covenant of Peace (5:17–20; 43–48)

"Do not think that I have come to abolish the law or the prophets." Jesus does not ask Jewish Christians to abandon their traditional cultural and religious practices. His teaching respects diversity but goes beyond it. "Unless your righteousness exceeds that of the scribes and Pharisees." These were respected teachers and models for many in the audience. However, Jesus will present a challenge to go even beyond them so they will not be tempted to return to their former teachers. He announces that he has not come to abolish but to *fulfill*, a word found seventeen times in Matthew, more than any other gospel. It does not mean fulfillment in a narrow or just predictive sense, but has the sense of perfection or completion. The goal is at the end of this section: "Be perfect, therefore, as your heavenly Father is perfect" (5:48). Perfection, or fullness, is one of the great meanings of peace. The Torah itself was called a covenant of peace. Jesus does not add to it, but goes deep into its inner nature as he proclaims his teaching on the Torah commandments that follows.

The Fifth Commandment: Anger and Murder (5:21–26)

"You have heard that it was said…but I say to you." "You have heard" refers to God's thunderous voice giving the Ten

Commandments on Mount Sinai. "I say to you" is now God's voice through Jesus providing a new inner basis and motivation behind the Ten Commandments. "You shall not murder" is the fifth commandment, which everyone knows. Yet hanging it up in every classroom is not sufficient to prevent killing and violence. Jesus immediately goes to the inner roots of murder and violence. The first root is a lack of meaningful personal relationships. So Jesus repeats the words, *your brother (and sister)*, some seven times in this chapter. The second root is anger. From the context, this is not just a passing feeling but a deep unresolved hatred in the heart. It comes to the surface in insulting words, lack of personal respect and sensitivity toward others. The same word for anger is found in the story of Cain and Abel. Cain was angry with his brother and let this feeling brood in his heart until it resulted in murder (Gen 4:1–16).

To resolve these causes of murder and violence, Jesus elevates forgiveness and peaceful reconciliation to the highest religious duty, more than a gift at the altar of the Temple that was usually a peace offering. This is illustrated by a humorous extreme: If an unresolved anger comes to a person's memory even in the middle of a religious ceremony, that person should immediately drop everything, go out, and seek a reconciliation. "Come to terms quickly with your accuser while you are on the way to court with him." Jesus advocates a Jewish tradition that opponents should take the long walk to a court case together. This was so people might dialogue, make their own terms, and not wait for a judge's decision that could be harsh and costly for everyone concerned.

The Sixth Commandment and Adultery (5:27–30)

The well-known sixth commandment likewise is not enough to curb sexual excesses. Jesus again goes to the inner roots, a lack of personal respect and relationship that regards another person as a mere object of pleasure. "Everyone who looks at a woman with lust has already committed adultery with her in his heart." This differs from thoughts or imagination. It is something deep in the heart and intention that moves toward the abusive actions next described: "If your right eye causes you to sin…or…if your right hand causes you to sin…." The remedy must be decisive and prompt: "tear it out…cut it off." These are typical oriental exaggerations, but they call for prompt action when facing occasions of sin. In Mark 9:46, we saw the limited reference to *gehenna*, or hell. However, the many references to future rewards and punishments in Matthew prompt us to believe that he wrote down Jesus' words in the sense of future punishment. (The teaching on divorce will be discussed later under household instructions.)

Eighth Commandment: Oaths and Swearing (5:33–37)

Here Jesus moves to the eighth commandment concerning false witness and untruth. Casuistry was popular in ancient times, and still today, in determining the boundaries between right and wrong. Jesus advocates a new language that does not rely on oaths and expletives to try to convince or impress others. "Let your word be 'Yes, Yes,' or 'No, No.'" Here again the inner cure is a trustfulness that relies on a simplicity of words and expressions. A truly "whole" person of peace speaks from the heart and can be "low key."

Peaceful Nonviolence and Retaliation

"An eye for an eye and a tooth for a tooth" comes from Exodus 21:24. Unfortunately, it has often been interpreted literally and out of context. Originally this law provided for a just legal recompense (usually in money or other exchange) instead of a terrible vengeance. Jesus responds, "Do not resist the evildoer." Jesus does not call for passivity but a spirit and direction of life that overcomes evil by good instead of retaliation. The expression "to turn the other cheek" has even entered the English language. It is meant to humorously express that we should not simply reply to evil with evil. Some of the humor in Jesus' words has been lost unless we translated his next expression by "If someone wants to sue you in court and take your coat, let that person take all your clothes also!" Jesus does not teach mere passivity, but "retaliating" with loving action.

"If anyone forces you to go one mile, go along the second." Everyone in the empire knew what it meant when Roman soldiers requisitioned civilians to carry their heavy baggage, often under the hot sun. The ordinary response at the end of the required mile was seething anger and at least a silent curse. The humorous response of "flower people" is to smile and say, "Could I help you for another mile." "Give to those who ask you." These are not polite beggars but rude pushy ones—a real test for cheerful generosity. We would like them to politely ask for favors, not press us with just demands for their human rights to food, clothing, and shelter. "Giving" is its own reward. Those who feel they are receiving justice, not favors, often do not express gratitude.

Love for One's Enemies

"You shall love your neighbor and hate your enemy." This is not in the Bible but is a common saying or proverb. Matthew's Gospel is very practical. What can be done with recurring, gnawing thoughts of hurtful people? The answer is simple and humorous: "Retaliate" by sending love and energy through prayer. Yet this is so difficult for weak human nature that Jesus provides a new resource: "that you may be children of your Father in heaven." This last statement is the central motivation of the Sermon on the Mount. *Children* here refer to those who are similar to and imitate their heavenly parent. The ideal then becomes possible because children can share their parents' power.

Imitation of God was the highest ideal of Jewish piety. Here it comes from watching God in nature bestow the gifts of sun and rain on everyone, despite their actions. God's love is unconditional—not based on a recipient's merit. The theme of love for the "good and bad" will continue through Matthew. This Gospel is concerned about practical application even in details. Greetings were very important in this culture. Much time was spent in stopping to talk, exchanging an embrace and kiss with family and friends. But Jesus points to more than tit for tat. What about taking the initiative to greet even strangers?

Be Perfect, Therefore, As Your Heavenly Father Is Perfect

This does not mean to be a "perfectionist." It means some-one who is continually growing and maturing as a real child of God. Growth involves learning through experience—which is a nice way of saying "through mistakes." This is the way that Peter and the apostles grew also. The Greek word for perfect is *teleios*. In the Greek, this sometimes translates the root *shalōm*, belong-ing to the *shalom* family of vocabulary. Being like God means becoming a person of peace, completeness, perfection. The high-est compliment in the Bible is to be called a "child of peace." In the Bible, God told David that he could not build the first Temple because he had shed too much blood and waged great wars. However, "See, a son shall be born to you; he shall be a *man of peace.* I will give him peace from all his enemies on every side; for his name shall be Solomon, and I will give peace and quiet to Israel in his days" (1 Chr 22:9). Even a little knowledge of Hebrew tells us that there is a play on sounds here along with a triple "peace." Peace is *shalom*, closely matching the sounds in *Solomon*.

Secrecy in Prayer, Charity, Fasting, and Possessions (6:1–34)

Jesus' concern for the inner basis of religion now goes to prayer, almsgiving, fasting, and money. Privacy was not easy to find in the small houses and crowded streets of ancient times. There was much public prayer as people stopped for required prayer during fixed times such as the hours of Temple sacrifice. In a world without banks, checkbooks, and credit cards, donations were placed in public collection boxes and were observed by many bystanders. Jesus says, "Do not let your left hand know what your right hand is doing." This is a comic paradox to express the neces-sity of not parading good works to win publicity or the esteem of others, "so that your alms may be done in secret and your Father who sees in secret will reward you."

The phrase *in secret (en tō cryptō)* occurs six times, four times immediately before the Lord's Prayer and twice right after it. Any ulterior motive such as being seen by others destroys the wholeness of a perfect gift to a perfect Father. The Lord's Prayer itself was a secret gift to the baptized. It was originally meant to be recited in an atmosphere of secrecy. The opening declaration is "Hallowed be *your* name," not *ours* or *mine*. Prayer needs this atmosphere of tranquility, another quality of peace. "If you forgive others their trespasses, your heavenly Father will also forgive you" (6:14). This is a commentary immediately after the Lord's Prayer. In the "divine Internet" the peace and forgiveness obtained from God occurs at the same time we give it to one another.

Fasting also accompanied the Our Father for many centuries. Prayer for the ancients was a total affair. Jesus presupposes this type of wholeness and intensity. People used bodily gestures such as raising their hands, lifting their eyes, and praying aloud. To give greater intensity to their prayer, they often fasted or gave up sleep. When this was exaggerated, they were quite a sad, though impressive sight. Jesus, laughingly, even advised his disciples to pretend to be feasting rather than fasting to avoid ostentation and people's good impressions.

Possessions and Intentions (6:19–24)

With no bank accounts in those days, people often hid money and precious goods under a house or in a wall in order to save for the future. But all material goods are perishable and according to biblical tradition, money spent for God's purposes mysteriously multiplies. Matthew's concern here and through his Gospel is totality and the heart's intention: "Where your treasure is there your heart will be also."

This is reinforced by the image of an eye in good focus. Good actions flow from sound eyes and vision, images of the heart. All this prepares for good decisions on money and possessions. Matthew likes to contrast two opposites for audience choice and involvement. Service to God is total by its nature and cannot survive along with worship of money. While we rarely use the term *Master*, the word *addict* is similar, coming from the root *dictator*. This is something or someone telling us what to do, and taking God's place.

Cures for Worry and Anxiety: A Way to Peace and Wholeness (6:25–34)

Continuing the wealth discussion, the reason why many people accumulate money is worry or fear for the future. Jesus' responses are: 1) "Is not life more than food?" Life itself comes from God as a gift and cannot be controlled. 2) "Look at the birds of the air.... Consider the lilies of the field." All of nature is a constant display of God's care for the least creature, whether plants or animals. 3) "Strive first for the kingdom of God." With this priority, everything else is viewed in perspective. As a result, we will later see that Paul declares, "The kingdom of God is not food and drink but righteousness and *peace* and joy in the Holy Spirit" (Rom 14:17). In conclusion Jesus declares, "Do not worry about tomorrow, for tomorrow will have worries of its own." The big secret is to live fully one day at a time. Over 90 percent of worries concern a tomorrow that does yet exist.

On Judging Others and Equality (7:1–5)

"Do not judge so that you may not be judged." In view of customary avoidance of God's name, the second part would be, "that God may not judge you." Preoccupation with criticizing others means taking God's place but lacking God's compassion and neglecting self-criticism. The attitude of searching for specks or flaws in others blinds our eyes from appreciating, like God, the good in others. In the biblical view of an interrelated world of harmony and peace, this unbalanced view must be corrected by God's intervention. All people enjoy a basic equality before God, as shown in the first creation account: "God created humankind in his image, in the image of God he created them; male and female he created them" (Gen 1:27). The psalmist refers to true equality in the image of a friend as a "man of my *shalom*" (41:9) or "my equal, my companion" (55:13). This passage is an important introduction to the coming final teaching of the Sermon on the Mount on the Golden Rule (7:12). It deals with the fundamental nonjudgment attitude basic to living in peace. People cannot be graded or categorized.

Obtaining Answers to Prayers—Equality and "Favoritism" for All (7:7–11)

"Ask, Search, Knock." Jesus uses a triple image and then repeats it in another form. In oral teaching, the more important anything is, the more often it is repeated. Perseverance and complete trust is the strong message: "Keep on asking; keep on searching; keep on knocking." "If you…know how to give good gifts to your children, how much more will your Father in heaven give good things." This is a central revelation of Jesus that God is kinder than any possible human parent, indeed kinder than all of them combined. God also treats his children equally and without favoritism. As such, Matthew's frequent mention of rewards and punishments must be seen in perspective. Jesus did not come on earth to teach about heaven and hell. This was already part of Jewish traditional teaching and is also found in other religions as well.

The Golden Rule (7:12)

"Do to others as you would have them do to you" is even found in the dictionary under *Golden Rule.* Jesus, however, made it into a summary of all religion. This Gospel is very insistent on "doing." This verb is repeated again and again, leading to a climax in the final judgment scene in 25:31–46. The last part, "As you would have them do to you," sums up Jesus' identification with others, another central Gospel theme. This moves toward the final Gospel teaching statement, in the Last Judgment scene: "Just as you did not do it to one of the least of these, you did not do it to me" (25:45).

In the sermon opening, Jesus had said that he had come to fulfill the law and the prophets (5:17). Now he announces that this Golden Rule is indeed that fulfillment with the words, "This is indeed the law and the prophets." To make absolutely sure this message is never forgotten, Matthew repeats it two other times in his Gospel: in the teaching on the greatest commandment (22:39–40) and his response to the rich young man (19:19). This is an early Christian teaching. Decades earlier, the apostle Paul had written, "The whole law is summed up in a single commandment, 'You shall love your neighbor as yourself'" (Gal 5:14).

Closing Decisions: Two Roads, Types of Teachers, Disciples, Households (7:13–27)

Of special interest in regard to peace are the kinds of disciples: those who considered themselves superior because of their charismatic gifts of prophecy, miracles, healings, exorcisms (21–23). At the judgment, Jesus will tell them, "I never knew you; go away from me, you evildoers." Any rankings of human invention destroy peace and harmony. Special gifts are not for personal aggrandizement but to help others. Jesus began his instruction with the image of a house filled with light. It closes also with a comparison between two types of houses: those built on rock and those built on sand. Without hearing and doing, discipleship lasts as long as a sand castle.

"Now when Jesus had finished saying these things." This is a literary ending. Similar statements conclude each of Matthew's five great discourses. "He taught them as having authority." Jesus is like Moses, but superior. This authority is a central issue in Matthew. It leads to the Gospel ending and a "graduation ceremony." There on a mountain platform Jesus will hand over this same teaching authority to others who will bring his teachings to the world accompanied by Jesus' presence and power.

Roots of the "Greatest Commandment"— Jesus' Identification with Others

We have seen that Jesus proclaimed the Golden Rule as summing up the law and prophets. However, this is much more than a neat summary or slogan. It was something he embodied in all he did through a deep empathy and identification with others. The roots of this are in the description of God's nature that prompted him to renew his "covenant of peace" with his people after they had broken it by worshiping the golden calf (Exod 34:19). Moses begged God to reveal himself and renew the covenant. In response, God pronounced the meaning of his revelation name *Yhwh*, first shown to Moses at the burning bush (Exod 3:14–15). In describing himself to Moses, the first word pronounced is that he is *rachum* (34:6). This is often translated "merciful," but it is more like a gut-rooted "womb-compassion" since it is derived from the word *rechem*, meaning "womb."

There are two primary ways that Matthew expresses this root quality of God. The first is through the use of the verb *splanknizomai*. This sounds like a Greek mouthful, but its root is even found in the English dictionary as *splanchnic*, referring to the nerve following the aorta down from the heart to carry the deepest feelings. The word is not used in ordinary parlance but is familiar to doctors and the scientific world. In Bibles, it is often translated by "having compassion." In the Greek world, it referred to the deepest, "gut," or visceral, feelings.

Matthew has this verb, particularly in regard to Jesus' miracles, more often than any other gospel. Like Moses, this notion of compassion is the root of Jesus' mission of peace. Before selecting the Twelve as his helpers, Jesus has *compassion* on the crowds because they were harassed and helpless like sheep without a shepherd (9:36). He has the same feeling for the hungry multitudes before each of the two feeding miracles (14:14; 15:32). In the parable of forgiveness of a great debt, the king has compassion on the debtor and forgives everything (18:27). In the last miracle before his entry into Jerusalem, two blind men ask him to open their eyes. The text notes, "Moved with compassion, Jesus touched their eyes. Immediately, they regained their sight and follow him" (20:34).

This compassion prompts Matthew to focus on Jesus' identification with others, especially the sick, as the essential second step to activating the Golden Rule of the Sermon on the Mount. We find examples of this in the healing miracles as Jesus identifies with Isaiah's Servant of the Lord. After the cure of Peter's mother-in-law, Matthew adds a summary of Jesus' healing ministry:

> That evening they brought to him many who were possessed with demons; and he cast out the spirits with a word, and cured all who were sick. This was to fulfill

what had been spoken through the prophet Isaiah, "He took our infirmities and bore our diseases." (8:16–17)

Matthew's quote from Isaiah 53:4 in this context describes Jesus as the Servant of the Lord who compassionately identifies with his people and takes upon himself their burdens. This will be confirmed and amplified in a later summary. In Matthew's Sabbath stories, Jesus is motivated by compassion. In the first, the disciples were hungry and plucking heads of grain as they walked through the fields. The Pharisees complain to Jesus, "Look, your disciples are doing what is not lawful to do on the Sabbath" (12:2). Jesus replies by recalling how King David gave precedence to mercy in allowing his soldiers to even eat the special loaves of presence within the Temple (1 Sam 21:1–6). Then Jesus said, "I tell you, something greater than the temple is here. But if you had known what this means, 'I desire mercy and not sacrifice,' you would not have condemned the guiltless" (12:6–7; Hos 6:6).

In a second Sabbath story, Jesus heals a man on the Sabbath, justifying himself by noting that compassion prompts people to help a trapped sheep on the Sabbath and saying, "How much more valuable is a human being than a sheep?" Jesus again quotes the prophet Hosea speaking in the name of God, "I desire mercy and not sacrifice" (Hos. 6:6). After this Matthew notes, "The Pharisees went out and conspired against him, how to destroy him" (12:14). The fact that Jesus is risking his life by making mercy a priority over every law prompts a second reference to the Servant of the Lord:

> When Jesus became aware of this, he departed. Many crowds followed him, and he cured all of them, and he ordered them not to make him known. This was to fulfill what had been spoken through the prophet Isaiah: "Here is my servant, whom I have chosen, my beloved, with whom my soul is well pleased. I will put my Spirit upon him, and he will proclaim justice to the Gentiles. He will not wrangle or cry aloud, nor will anyone hear his voice in the streets. He will not break a bruised reed or quench a smoldering wick until he brings justice to

victory. And in his name the Gentiles will hope."
(12:19–21; Isaiah 42:1–4)

Mercy to the Outcast and Marginalized

Matthew continues his theme of merciful identification in other areas. Both Mark and Luke relate the story of Jesus' call of the unpopular tax collector Levi (2:14 and 5:29–32). Matthew has obviously the same story but with his own name inserted: "As Jesus was walking along, he saw a man called Matthew sitting at the tax booth; and he said to him, 'Follow me.' And he got up and followed him" (9:9). Is this the author's way of identifying with the tax collector and inviting the Gospel audience to do so also? When Jesus then had dinner with tax collectors and sinners, the Pharisees objected, since these people were obviously unclean due to their occupation or contact with Gentiles. Jesus replies (as in Mark and Luke), "Those who are well have no need of a physician, but those who are sick." However, only Matthew adds the text from Hosea 6:6 when Jesus says, "Go out and learn what this means: 'I desire mercy and not sacrifice'" (9:13).

The theme of welcome for the marginalized reaches a high point during Jesus' symbolic cleansing of the Temple. At that time, "[t]he blind and the lame came to him in the temple, and he cured them" (21:14). These were people considered unclean because of handicaps mentioned specifically in Leviticus 21:16–21. Jesus' action shows that the "house of prayer" (Matthew does not have "all the nations") will be a place where the marginalized and outcasts will be welcomed.

Jesus' Final Teaching on Identification in the Judgment Scene

Jesus' final teachings before the events leading to his passion and death are found in Matthew's chapters 24 and 25. Central to these is a final judgment scene where all the nations are gathered together before Jesus, the Son of Man. He separates the people into two parts, the sheep on his right and the goats on his left. Then he says to those on his right hand:

Come, you that are blessed by my Father, inherit the kingdom prepared for you from the foundation of the world; for I was hungry and you gave me food, I was thirsty and you gave me something to drink, I was a stranger and you welcomed me, I was naked and you gave me clothing, I was sick and you took care of me, I was in prison and you visited me. (25:34–36)

The just are surprised that the judgment seems already accomplished and ask, "When was it that we saw you hungry and gave you food, thirsty and gave you something to drink...." repeating all that Jesus has said to them. This repetition seems unnecessary to modern ears, but it is Matthew's way in oral teaching to show how important something is by presenting it again and again. In all, there are four repetitions as those on the left side hear the same words of Jesus in a negative sense and reply in like manner. The king responds to each group by a solemn amen statement, first to the just, "Amen I say to you, just as you did it to one of the least of these who are members of my family (literally, "my brothers") you did it to me" (25:40). Then to those on the left hand, "Amen I say to you, as long as you did not do it to one of the least of these, you did not do it to me" (25:45).

The scene above is really a final practical summary of Jesus' triple presentation of love of neighbor (5:12; 19:19; 22:38–39) as the fulfillment of the law and the prophets. In the last of these, 22:38–39, love of neighbor is connected with love of God in the *Shemah*. This is because identification with Jesus in love of neighbor is really imitation and love of God. All through the Gospel of Matthew, from Jesus' baptism onward, Matthew presents Jesus as the Son of God, seven times in all. Jesus' mission of social justice through his preaching of repentance, his care for the sick and outcasts, the poor, hungry, homeless, strangers, and prisoners is the model for the Gospel audience in fulfilling the law and the prophets.

Rebuilding a House of Peace—Jesus' Household Instructions (19:1–29)

We use the term *house of peace* in view of Jesus' instructions to the Twelve when they enter a house during their missionary journey: "As you enter the house, greet it. If the house is worthy, let your peace come upon it" (10:12). The common greeting was "Peace be with you" or "Peace to this house."

This greeting from a messenger of God carries his presence, and when it is received, the house becomes God's house, a house of peace. Jesus' household instructions are very important. They present the necessary means of breaking down the patriarchal domination or ranks of prominence that are obstacles to a true house of peace. The head of the household, *oikodespotēs* or *pater-familias*, was the powerful patriarchal ruler of the household in the Jewish and Roman world. He is named seven times in Matthew, more than the other gospels together.

In the opening pages of this chapter, we have already seen how important this household economic and family head was in Matthew's affluent households. First of all, women, especially wives and daughters, were under strict control of the household head and patriarchal laws regarding marriage and divorce. For reference, we will print part of the instruction below.

Marriage and Divorce (19:3–9)

Some Pharisees came to him, and to test him they asked, "Is it lawful for a man to divorce his wife for any cause?" He answered, "Have you not read that the one who made them at the beginning 'made them male and female,' and said, 'For this reason a man shall leave his father and mother and be joined to his wife, and the two shall become one flesh'? So they are no longer two, but one flesh. Therefore what God has joined together, let no one separate." They said to him, "Why then did Moses command us to give a certificate of dismissal and to divorce her?" He said to them, "It was because you were so hard-hearted that Moses allowed you to divorce your wives, but from the beginning it was not so. And I say to you, whoever divorces his wife, except for unchastity, and marries another commits adultery." (19:3–9)

This "command" of Moses, found in Deuteronomy 24:1, allows a husband to give his wife a written notice of dismissal and send her away. Jesus' answer appeals to the first creation account where God creates man and woman *equally* in the divine image (Gen 1:27). Here we have the only reference in the Bible, outside of Genesis, to this text in the first creation account (chapters 1—2:4). All other references to woman's creation build on the second account beginning in 2:4. There she is formed from the first man and dependent on him. In this account the man gives names to all the animals and to the woman also (Gen 2:19–23). He calls her "woman" because she has the same flesh and was taken out of "man" (2:23). Then the text follows, "Therefore a man leaves his father and his mother and clings to his wife, and they become one flesh" (2:24). However, in Jesus' answer there is a remarkable piece of exegesis. This last verse is only in the second creation account but Jesus moves it to follow the first declaration of creation as male and female equally in the divine image (1:27). Thus, Jesus states that a personal covenant of man and woman follows from God's creation in making them both equally made in the divine image, not from the woman's similarity to and origin from the man! Therefore, there can be no patriarchal right of a man to dismiss his wife as an unequal subordinate.

Father and Children (19:13–15)

Children were in the lowest household rung of hierarchy, just above slaves. They had no one to whom they could go for defense of their rights. So it is not surprising that the male disciples exercise their patriarchal "rights" to chase away and rebuke women who were bringing their children to Jesus that he might touch them (with a blessing):

Then little children were being brought to him in order that he might lay his hands on them and pray. The disciples spoke sternly to those who brought them; but

Jesus said, "Let the little children come to me, and do not stop them; for it is to such as these that the kingdom of heaven belongs." And he laid his hands on them and went on his way.

Jesus completely reverses the position of children from the lowest to the highest rank. The teaching on children really starts with the literary enclosure in 18:1–4:

At that time the disciples came to Jesus and asked, "Who is the greatest in the kingdom of heaven?" He called a child, whom he put among them, and said, "Truly I tell you, unless you change and become like children, you will never enter the kingdom of heaven. Whoever becomes humble like this child is the greatest in the kingdom of heaven. Whoever welcomes one such child in my name welcomes me."

In the above texts, Jesus changes the position of a child from the least or last to the greatest. They are models for those who wish to enter the kingdom. In addition, he identifies with them as one who deliberately chooses to be as a child in his service of others. Those who receive children receive Jesus himself. The image of a child introduces a whole chapter (18) on the priority of "little ones" in the kingdom. The focus is on the child's flexibility to change. This means new beginnings and repentance that will now be applied to various community situations. Other child sayings complete the child image and model. Temptations or abuse of these little ones is the most serious sin of all. They are so important that "their angels continually see the face of my Father in heaven." Only Matthew has this traditional Jewish teaching on guardian angels, found especially in the Book of Tobit.

Care for the Community of Little Ones (18:6–35)

Next follows the emphasis on the special care for lost little ones. The first example of lost little ones is found in the lost sheep parable, which illustrates Jesus' own approach of going to the lost sheep of the tribe of Israel (see 10:6). First, the lost ones must be a real community priority as shown by a diligent *search* for someone who is lost or has left the community. Then follows the joyful community celebration when someone is found and welcomed back into the community. "It is not the will of your Father in heaven that one of these little ones be lost." The community search embodies God's own concern; the finding is God's own finding. This joyful reconciliation is a special part of true peace.

Lost Brothers and Sisters Are Also the Little Ones (18:15–35)

The situation is this: Someone attending community worship gatherings has seriously and publicly offended another member. However, the person remains unrepentant, as if nothing has happened. This is a dangerous matter because every Christian is a repentant sinner by definition, saved now from future judgment by honesty and truth. God's future judgment awaits a hypocrite. The way to approach such a person is with great gentleness, sensitivity, and secrecy (at first) with a humble, helping attitude: "Go and point out the fault when the two of you are alone."

Only if this does not succeed should stronger means be taken—a small private group of two or three witnesses. If this fails, then as a final desperate resort: "Tell it to the church." If this is in vain, "only then let such a one be to you as a Gentile and a tax collector." These are typical Jewish expressions for someone excluded from community meetings. The intention is medicinal not punitive—temporary exclusion from community privileges so he or she can realize the harm done, and then return in repentance to be joyfully received back into the community as the lost sheep in the above parable. This is the root of the sacrament of reconciliation in its original community atmosphere.

"Whatever you bind on earth will be bound in heaven." The church community's forgiveness is ratified by God in heaven. The concluding sayings show that this is because of Jesus' presence and power in the church. The word *church* is only found in 18:17 and in 16:18, concerning Peter's role as teacher.

What About Forgiveness for Continual Backsliders? *(18:21–35)*

The next group comprises continual backsliders. Just how far can a community go in forgiving those who are continually falling and then trying to come back? This is the humorous question of Peter, representing church authority's worries about this matter: "How often should I forgive? As many as seven times?" Peter thought he was doing very well. The number seven symbolizes a full and appropriate amount. However, God's forgiveness is foolish and extravagant by human standards: seventy-seven times.

The illustrative parable that follows is really the Lord's Prayer petition in story form: "Forgive us our debts as we also have forgiven our debtors." The ten thousand talents, representing debts to God, is enormous enough to require a hundred reincarnations or more to pay off. The verb translated *forgive* is from the Greek root *charis*, and thus is an action of favor, grace, and love.

The debt of a fellow servant to this man was infinitesimal in comparison, yet he threw his friend into prison. The other slaves (community members) are deeply distressed by such action and report it to the king. The king then handed him over to the torturers (to find out where he had hidden his money), for he had been deceptive in saying he could not pay. The ending of the story and its emphasis on the heart illustrate the genuineness and sincerity that real forgiveness should have.

Household Economics and Peace (20:1–16)

The story of the rich young man has already been discussed in the last chapter. However, the parable on the laborers in the vineyard is only in Matthew 20:1–16. It is really part of household instructions as pertaining to economics by sharing and overturning householder business values. At a critical time for his vineyard grape harvest, a landowner must hire a large number of day workers to quickly complete the required work. Unsure of how many men will be needed, he prudently begins hiring early with a minimum team so he can later hire more if needed. After agreeing with them for the usual sufficient wage of a denarius a day, he sent them into his vineyard. As the day progresses, he discovers he needs more workers and goes out to hire them at nine o'clock, noon, and even at five. Those at this last hour have only an hour to work before sunset and darkness. The owner made no contract with the later workers but only promised, "I will pay you whatever is just."

At sunset, according to biblical law, the landowner instructed his manager to pay the workers, beginning with those who came at five. This gave the earlier workers the opportunity to observe the process and react to it. Also it prepared for the concluding statement and meaning of the parable:

> Now when those hired at five o'clock came, each of them received a denarius. Now when the first came, they thought they would receive more; but each of them also received a denarius. And when they received it they grumbled against the householder, saying, "These last have worked only one hour, and you have made them *equal* to us, who have borne the burden of the day and the scorching heat." (9–12)

The household manager replied in a kindly manner, "Friend, I am doing you no injustice; did you not agree with me for a denarius?... I choose to give this last the same as I give to you.... Are you envious because I am generous?" Most interpretation has emphasized the householder's generosity, but if this were true he should have given more to those who worked so hard for many more hours. Instead, the central matter is that the landowner wants "to do what is *just*." This means that, regardless of the fact that some workers labored only an hour, they still need a full daily wage to feed, clothe, and care for their families. The complaint, "You have made them *equal* to us," actually expresses what the owner is trying to do—promote true equality in his temporary household family of workers. But in doing so, at added expense, he is subverting the typical household goal of acquiring more wealth—which would entail cutting costs, especially the salaries of poor workers. We can see why Matthew repeats his favorite expression as his "upside-down" theology: "So the last will be first and the first last" (20:16). A household of peace and justice—which always go together—subverts ordinary patriarchal household values.

Wholeness, Peace,
and Community in Matthew

Peace is always complete in a community, not within individuals alone. Matthew is the great community Gospel. We have already seen the strong image of *house* in the Sermon on the Mount. At Jesus' farewell supper he made a covenant of peace with a community as he asked his disciples to share his bread and instructed them about the cup, "Drink from it all of you, this is my blood of the covenant" (26:28). He promises he will only drink it again *with you* (plural) in his Father's kingdom. Matthew is called the *church* Gospel, the only gospel with this word, *ekklēsia* (16:18; 18:18). This word is used in the Greek Old Testament for the assembly of God's people. It is now the place for the special presence of Jesus: "Where two or three are gathered in my name, I am there among them" (18:20).

To enhance this community aspect, Matthew makes some changes in the stories of Jesus' miracles. Both Mark and Luke have the cure of a blind man, once on a separate occasion and again before Jesus' entry into Jerusalem. Matthew instead has the cure of two blind men, both in 9:27–30 and in 20:29–33.

In addition, he has two demoniacs (8:28) in the same story where Mark has only one (5:1–20). He invites the Gospel audience to join in the community chorus of the blind men's praise: "Lord, have mercy on us" (20:30)—*Kyrie eleēson*, the favorite mantra of the church that has continued for almost two thousand years. At the death of Jesus, not only the centurion proclaims Jesus as God's son, but *those with him* (27:54).

The Passion Story and the Messiah
of Peace and Nonviolence

The passion account contains the oldest material in the Gospel. Everything else leads to it. Consequently, the image of Jesus presented there is a primary one. Here we will not duplicate Mark, but present additional aspects introduced by Matthew in regard to a Messiah of Peace and nonviolence. At Jesus' arrest, the gospels relate that one of the group (Peter, in John's Gospel) immediately drew his sword in violent defense, wounding one of the arresters. Matthew records Jesus' protest and order to cease, "Put your sword back into its place; for all who take the sword will perish by the sword. Do you think that I cannot appeal to my Father, and he will at once send me more than twelve legions of angels? But how then would the scriptures be fulfilled, which say it must happen in this way?" (26:52–54).

With these words, Jesus announced the general principal that all violence only breeds more violence and ultimately destroys those who rely on it. At the same time, Jesus is not a helpless victim of power. There is another deeper power he can call upon. The reference to scripture recalls that there is a hidden plan of God at work for those who follow the way of peace. Then, as in Mark, Jesus contrasts his peaceful open teaching in the Temple to their action coming to him secretly with swords and clubs. They are the violent ones, not he. In Matthew, this takes the form of an announcement to the crowds at that very hour. Matthew also adds a second reference to the fulfillment of God's plans in the scriptures.

Only Matthew has the detailed story of Judas' death, for an important reason. Judas had gone to the governing authorities to plan the arrest of a violent messianic contender (26:14–16). But once Judas realized that Jesus was condemned, he repented and brought back his contract price to the chief priests and declared, "I have sinned in betraying innocent blood" (27:4). In the Bible, the greatest crime is that of shedding *innocent blood*, mentioned twenty-two times in the Bible and an essential part of God's covenant of peace. This crime is so great that it pollutes the whole land and takes away the peace and harmony of creation. Consequently, this guilt must be purged and the only way described is through taking the life of the person responsible (Num 35:30–34).

The chief priests and elders, however, will not take back the money, nor take any responsibility themselves, but tell Judas, "What is that to us? See to it yourself" (27:5). So Judas flung down the money and went away to hang himself. Immediately, a modern reader might reason that it was wrong for him to take his own life. But in the scriptures, a suicide at times can be the most honorable response to make. For example, King Saul took his life when surrounded and wounded by his enemies (1 Sam 31:4–6). Judas, since the authorities would not punish him and purge the land from guilt, took it upon himself. Thus he became a witness that Jesus was not guilty of being a violent revolutionary but a Messiah of peace. What follows Judas' death seems to further indicate the positive result of Judas' death. The priests took the money and used it to buy a field as a burial place for strangers. In this way, Judas' death appears as a shadow of Jesus' death, which culminates in the gospel mission to all the nations (28:19). With all this in mind, Judas dies more like a hero than a villain.

A second affirmation of Jesus as innocent comes from the special intervention of God in the form of a disturbing dream of Pilate's wife. As the governor was on the judgment seat, ready for a decision, she sent a message to him, "Have nothing to do with this just man, for today I have suffered a great deal because of a dream about him" (27:19). Even the reverberations of impending innocent blood disturb the peace of the whole inner world. A third sign, likewise only in Matthew, appears when Pilate washed his hands in public, saying, "I am innocent of this man's blood; see to it yourselves" (27:24). These last words, but in the singular, are the same as those of the chief priest and elders to Judas.

Matthew, in a parallel to Judas, notes that they did "see to it themselves." He writes, "Then the people as a whole answered, 'His blood be on us and on our children'" (27:25). The phrase "His blood be on us" is a way of saying, "We take responsibility." The phrase "the people as a whole," literally, "all the people," can only refer to the limited crowd that was shouting for crucifixion due to the incitement and persuasion of the chief priests and elders (27:20). Matthew calls these latter, "the chief priests and elders *of the people*," four times (21:23; 26:3,47,25). Theoretically, they were supposed to represent the people as the ruling authority. But in practice, the chief priests were appointed by Rome, and they, most likely, in turn chose elders who would support them as puppets of Rome.

Actually, Pilate could not merely throw off his responsibility to others. He takes action as "he released Barabbas for them; after flogging Jesus, he handed him over to be crucified" (27:26). Flogging was usually a preliminary step to crucifixion. In the next verse, Pilate's soldiers come to take Jesus away to the governor's praetorium where they make sport of Jesus and mock him as "King of the Jews." Matthew adds to Mark's description by noting that the soldiers stripped Jesus of his own clothing before this. Also he adds that the soldiers put a reed in Jesus' hand as a mock staff of authority. Then they would take it from his hand and hit him over the head with it (27:31). Finally, "they led him away to crucify him."

On the cross, Matthew turns the mock title "King of the Jews" into a title of King of peace and life, in the sense of wholeness and completion. Only Matthew notes the divine intervention at Jesus' death of an earthquake that heralds not only Jesus' resurrection to new life, but also that of others:

> At that moment the curtain of the temple was torn in two, from top to bottom. The earth shook, and the rocks were split. The tombs also were opened, and many bodies of the saints who had fallen asleep were raised. After his resurrection they came out of the tombs and entered the holy city and appeared to many. (27:51–53)

Mark's Gospel ended with the angels commanding the women to tell Peter and the disciples that Jesus was to go ahead of them into Galilee as good shepherd. However, Matthew will add to this in order to see Jesus' message to completion: Jesus also appears to some women with the message to tell his brothers that they are to go ahead into Galilee where they will see him. The eleven disciples eventually do so and go to a mountain where Jesus appears to them and announces that he has received full authority over heaven and earth. With this authority he tells them to go out to all the nations, making disciples, baptizing and teach all that he has previously given them. Only in doing so will the Gospel message bring completeness, peace, and healing as the barriers separating the ancient world are broken down.

Summary Points for Praxis, Teaching and Ministry

- "Blessed are the Peacemakers" (5:9) is a "trademark" for the Sermon on the Mount in Matthew. The word *peacemaker* is found nowhere else in the Bible. Jesus calls them "children of God" for they are most like God who alone is shalom. The Sermon on the Mount provides a practical guide for peacemakers who are needed today more and more as the world becomes a great battleground. The worst occupation force is made up of those opponents or enemies that take up the precious space of our minds. Jesus' weapon is to pray for them and thus "get rid of" them each time they try to take over. Jesus' view of the Ten Commandments stresses their inner motivating force, which is a real compassion and the view of others as real brothers and sisters.

- The secret to obtaining this compassion is identification with how others feel, and the actions that flow accordingly. This leads to a deeper understanding and practice of the Golden Rule that only Matthew repeats three times in his Gospel as summing up all of religion. The importance of this identification with others is brought out in the final judgment scene with its sixfold repetition (in various forms) of the theme, "Amen I say to you, just as you did it to one of the least of these who are members of my family you did it to me" (25:40).

- Matthew's Gospel has a very special place for children both in the community and in the liturgy. Only this Gospel remembers their presence in Jesus' multiplication of loaves (14:21; 15:38). The children salute Jesus in the Temple, singing, "Hosanna to the Son of David." The Pharisees call upon Jesus to rebuke them, but he praises them as instruments of God (21:16–17). Jesus places a child in their midst as a humble model for members of the community in their relations to one another (18:2–5).

- Matthew is preeminently the Teacher's Gospel. The ending of the Gospel is like a graduation scene for qualified teachers. They have received the tradition of Jesus' sacred words in the Sermon on the Mount and the other Gospel discourses. They also receive Jesus' own authority as they hand on these words to others with Jesus' commission, "Go and make disciples of all nations." With this authority, they embody Jesus' own presence: "I am with you always." Thus Jesus' word becomes their word as they teach others.

4

THE GOSPEL OF LUKE: "PEACE ON EARTH"—ROOTS AND PRACTICE OF PEACE AND NONVIOLENCE

John the Baptist—"...to guide our feet in the way of peace" (1:79)

In describing John's role, Luke provides a valuable outline of the main peace themes in his Gospel. The very first words, after the dedication to Theophilus, read, "In the days of King Herod of Judea, there was a priest named Zechariah, who belonged to the priestly order of Abijah. His wife was a descendant of Aaron, and her name was Elizabeth." The mention of Herod has an ominous tone of a king who would surely oppose any rival. This Herod was Herod the Great, who ruled from 37 to 4 BC. Rome supported him as "King of the Jews," a puppet king of Judea. Herod the Great in turn was the father of Herod Antipas, who ruled over Galilee at the time of Jesus' ministry. By this time, Pontius Pilate had become the direct governor of Judea and ruled from AD 26 to 36. The mention of Herod the Great at the Gospel beginning foreshadows the role of Herod Antipas as the opposing force to the Baptist and his mission of peace.

The Birth of the Baptist: His Future Role as a Guide to Peace

To this day in Israel *shalom* is the common greeting whether personal, by letter, or on the telephone. Luke's Gospel contains the word in Greek, *eirēnē*, fourteen times, more than all the other gospels combined. It is also a leading theme in Jesus' preaching. Luke has Peter describe Jesus' ministry in the Acts of the Apostles when he declares that God sent Jesus to Israel "preaching peace" (10:36).

In itself, *shalom* has a broad range of meaning in the area of wholeness, well-being, harmony, completion, and fulfillment. Proceeding from these roots are many branches of meaning such as reconciliation, forgiveness, avoidance of conflict, and healing. The author and source of peace is God, who spreads this peace through an interconnected universe. Every greeting is really a prayer for peace, whether God's name is directly there or not. So we will not be surprised to find the preeminence of peace in the Baptist's story. This begins with predictions of his extraordinary birth and role. These predictions are confirmed by unusual signs.

First of all, his parents were beyond the usual ages of child-bearing and child rearing: "They had no children because Elizabeth was barren and both were getting on in years" (1:7). Second, Zechariah was chosen by lot to offer incense in the Temple building on the altar facing the veiled entrance to the Holy of Holies. Such a great privilege for a priest might not even occur in a lifetime. The fact that he was chosen by lot pointed to special divine intervention, according to views of that time. Next, he had a terrifying vision of an angel standing beside the altar of incense. But even more awesome was the announcement that he and his aged wife would have a child and that even his name, John, was designated. The announcement of any coming child, of course, would be a shock. But that their child would initiate a turning point in history like the great Elijah was simply overwhelming:

> He will turn many of the people of Israel to the Lord their God. With the spirit and power of Elijah, he will go before him, to turn the hearts of parents to their children, and the disobedient to the wisdom of the righteous, to make ready a people prepared for the Lord. (1:16–17)

The above verses are the final words of Malachi, the last written prophet of the Hebrew Bible. God promises that he will send the prophet Elijah again before the last day of the Lord. His role will be to "turn the hearts of parents to their children and the hearts of children to their parents" (4:5–6). This "turning to God" is expressed in Luke by the word *metanoia*, from the root "to change one's mind." Later, Luke will relate that "the word of God came to John son of Zechariah in the wilderness. He went into all the region around the Jordan, proclaiming a baptism of repentance *(metanoia)* for the forgiveness of sins" (3:2–3). This metanoia is mentioned nine times in his Gospel and five times in the Acts of the Apostles. Here again, Luke mentions it more than the other gospels combined. It becomes the real basis for true peace.

Zechariah was so shaken by the apparition and these words that he could not *believe* them. He said to the angel, "How will I know this is so? For I am an old man and my wife is getting on in years" (1:19). The angel Gabriel replied that Zechariah would be "mute, unable to speak, until the day that these things occur." Meanwhile, all the people outside were waiting for him to emerge from the Temple and wondered at the delay. They were waiting for the customary blessing of the priest. This blessing was a transfer of the divine energies to the people in response to the incense offering of themselves and their prayer. When Zechariah came out with only gestures, they knew he would not be able to pronounce the climactic priestly blessing. The words for this blessing were given directly by God to Moses: "Thus shall you bless the Israelites: You shall say to them, 'The LORD bless you and keep you; The LORD make his face to shine upon you, and be gracious to you; The LORD lift up his countenance upon you, and give you peace'" (Num 6:23–26).

The triple use of the name LORD, stands for the great revelation name YHWH given to Moses at the burning bush near Sinai (Exod 3:14–15). In reverence, all the people would bow each time that sacred name was pronounced so they would bring God's presence, power, and peace upon themselves. Luke starts his Gospel with the disappointing failure to receive the anticipated blessing of peace because of the lack of Zechariah's faith. Later we will see that Luke closes his Gospel with Jesus ascending into heaven and giving his disciples and Gospel audience the full priestly blessing of peace.

Elizabeth Takes the Initiative of Faith

This woman is the first to believe the good news, like the first women to believe in Jesus' resurrection at the empty tomb (24:8). Luke knows that the world can never have shalom in the sense of fullness without the equal presence and witness of women. Consequently, Luke's Gospel is often called the Gospel of Women. After Elizabeth gave birth, the family gathered eight days later for his circumcision and naming. The male-dominated group wanted to name the boy after his father. However, Elizabeth alone strongly objected and said, "No; he is to be called John" (1:60). However, the relatives persisted, "None of your relatives have this name." Then they made hand signs to Zechariah to win his support. He signaled for a writing tablet and scribbled, "His name is John." Everyone was amazed at this answer. For Zechariah it was a great leap of faith, as he finally trusted in the angel's apparition and message. Suddenly he could talk again and began to praise God. Luke writes that "Zechariah was filled with the Holy Spirit and spoke this prophecy." In it, Zechariah expanded on the future role of his son, the Baptist:

> You, child, will be called the prophet of the Most High; for you will go before the Lord to prepare his ways, to give knowledge of salvation to his people by the forgiveness of their sins. By the tender mercy of our God, the dawn from on high will break upon us, to give light to those who sit in darkness and in the shadow of death, *to guide our feet into the way of peace.* (1:76–79)

Zechariah explains where this "guide into the way of peace" will proceed from. The source is "the tender mercy of our God," sometimes translated "the compassion of our God." In Greek, it is the *splangchna* of the mercy of God. This, we have already seen, means literally the "viscera" or "gut feelings" of God, proceeding from his nature of *rachum* in Hebrew, "womb compassion," from the root *rechem*, meaning "womb." We will see this especially when we come to Luke's Sermon on the Plain. In it, Jesus announces the core of his teaching: "Be merciful, as your Father is merciful" (6:36). In Zechariah's words, this loving compassion arises from God each day like the morning sunrise with its warmth and light.

The Baptist's Ministry and the Way of Peace

Luke first contrasts the Baptist with the powerful authority structures at the time he began his ministry:

> In the fifteenth year of the reign of Emperor Tiberius, when Pontius Pilate was governor of Judea, and Herod was ruler of Galilee, and his brother Philip ruler of the region of Ituraea and Trachonitis, and Lysanias ruler of Abilene, during the high priesthood of Annas and Caiaphas, the word of God came to John son of Zechariah in the wilderness. (3:1–2)

The Herod above is the son of Herod the Great, who was king at the time of the birth of Jesus. Herod Antipas became the ruler of Galilee, while Pontius Pilate (AD 26–36) assumed direct Roman government of Judea. Caiaphas succeeded Annas. Both were the chief priests and Israel's leaders under Rome's appointment each year. The puppet King Herod and Pilate were very concerned to maintain the external Pax Romana. Although the Baptist advocated inner peace and change, Roman authorities were very wary of any popular movement attracting large crowds of people and stimulating hopes for national Jewish restoration.

The name of Herod begins and closes the account of the Baptist's ministry. Luke summarizes by writing that John proclaimed good news to the people. "But Herod the ruler, who had been rebuked by him because of Herodias, his brother's wife, and because of all the evil things that Herod had done, added to them all by shutting up John in prison" (3:19–20). Imprisonment was usually a prelude to execution. Both Mark 6:14–29 and Matthew 14:1–12 relate the story of John's death. He was a true prophet because he dared to rebuke even the king at the risk of his life. Jesus will follow the same path and challenge his disciples to do so also. Although a Messiah of Peace, Jesus does not hesitate to take strong stands against evil even at the risk of his life.

A Call to Repentance, Metanoia

"The word of God came to John, son of Zechariah, in the wilderness" (3:3). The opening phrase, "The word of God came," is the very same as that of Jeremiah (1:4) and other prophets in the Bible. John the Baptist culminates a line of great prophets through the centuries as mouthpieces of God: "He [John] went into all the region around the Jordan, proclaiming a baptism of repentance *(metanoia)* for the forgiveness of sins" (3:3). John's baptism and preaching aroused great excitement as the news spread everywhere that a new prophetic voice had arisen. Ordinarily, a baptism was required only of Gentile converts to Judaism. For these converts it meant starting an entirely new life and covenant with God as if they were newborn children. In this new life, all the past had to be carefully sifted. This was true of marriages, relationships, friendships, associations, and even their professions or work. All this was required before admission to God's covenant with the symbolic ceremony of circumcision.

In addition, John preached that, even for Jews, their circumcision was not an automatic guarantee of God's favor. John announced that because of the "wrath to come" (3:7) a new beginning and conversion was required. The description, "wrath to come," was a way of describing a coming great judgment of God. John warned the crowds who came to him: "You brood of vipers! Who warned you to flee from the wrath to come? Bear fruits worthy of repentance" (3:8).

It is likely that John was influenced by the practices of the Qumran ascetic Essene community living near the Jordan River. Initiates entered that community with a baptism in water and renewed this frequently. They vowed complete obedience to the Torah, adding an oath to share their possessions. However, John's baptism was once and for all in view of the coming kingdom. As a youth, the Baptist "was in the wilderness [desert] until the day he appeared publicly to Israel" (1:80). There he could have learned about the Qumran community or even have been associated with it.

The holy life of John and his disciples was an attracting magnet for others, a guide to the way of peace. The angel Gabriel had told Zechariah his father that John "must never drink wine or strong drink; even before his birth he will be filled with the Holy

Spirit" (1:15). Abstention from alcohol was one of the require-ments for Nazarite vows (Num 6:1–21). However, these were temporary, not permanent, like that of the Baptist. Also, Nazarites were forbidden cut their hair or shave during this time. As a result, artists have often pictured the Baptist as a Nazarite with long flowing hair as a sign of dedication to God.

Luke's Gospel has other references to John's holy and asce-tic life. His example introduces Jesus' teaching of the Lord's Prayer: "As he [Jesus] was praying in a certain place, and after he had finished, one of his disciples said to him, 'Lord, teach us to pray, as John taught his disciples'" (11:1). John the Baptist com-bined his ministry of preaching with prayers and taught others to do the same. The disciples shared a common life and helped John in his baptismal ministry.

On another occasion, Luke describes an objection some opponents raised about Jesus' disciples: "John's disciples, like the disciples of the Pharisees, frequently fast and pray, but your disci-ples eat and drink" (5:33). In the story of the tax collector and a Pharisee, Jesus describes the Pharisee who stood up to pray to God with the words, "I fast twice a week" (18:12). Fasting often went together with intense prayer because it absorbed all the body energies and focused them on God. The above descriptions all point to an austere image of the Baptist and a strict ascetic life. Many people considered him an extremist. Jesus declared, "John has come eating no bread and drinking no wine, and you say, 'He has a demon'; the Son of Man has come eating and drinking and you say, 'Look, a glutton and a drunkard, a friend of tax collectors and sinners'" (7:33–34). Nevertheless, Jesus paid the Baptist a great tribute when he told his disciples, "What then did you go out to see? A prophet? Yes, I tell you, and more than a prophet" (7:26).

Justice, Mercy, and Metanoia

In general, the practice of justice and mercy was the essence of metanoia. Since John's call was similar to Isaiah's, whom Luke names (3:4), the verses that follow are from Isaiah, the great prophet of justice. Luke also merits the title of being a Gospel of Justice. Peace and justice cannot be separated. The psalmist writes, "Justice and peace shall kiss one another" (85:11). Peace means wholeness and thus it cannot exist where justice is lacking, and justice by its very nature produces peace. Hence, Isaiah will declare, "The effect of justice will be peace, and the result of righteousness, quietness and trust forever" (32:17). Luke provides particular examples of this justice in John's preaching as an invitation to baptism:

> And the crowds asked him, *"What then should we do?"* In reply he told them very definitely, "Whoever has two coats must share with anyone who has none; and whoever has food must do likewise." Even tax collectors came to be baptized, and they asked him, "Teacher, *what should we do?*" He told them, "Collect no more than the amount prescribed for you." Soldiers also asked him, "And we, *what should we do?*" He told them also, "Do not extort money from anyone by threats or false accusation, and be satisfied with your wages." (3:10–15)

The triple repetition above of "what should we do?" is italicized to highlight the practical decisions essential to metanoia. The first is broad and general in the generous sharing of food and clothing. This introduces Luke's Gospel focus on justice. Then follows an answer to people considered the most "hopeless" groups for conversion. These were men who cooperated with the Roman government in the office of hated tax collectors. The Baptist does not ask them to abandon their scribal profession but to cheat no one, instead of heaping up money by overcharging people. Even soldiers are not asked to throw down their weapons but to relinquish violence by not using their power to extort money or to gain other advantages.

This focus on "what shall we do?" in response to preaching and metanoia also appears in Luke's Acts of the Apostles. After Peter addressed the crowds on the first Pentecost, they were deeply moved and asked, "What shall we do?" (2:38). Peter answered, "Repent, and be baptized every one of you in the name of Jesus Christ so that your sins may be forgiven; and you will receive the gift of the Holy Spirit." These practical consequences directly parallel the first response of the Baptist in regard to food and clothing: "All who believed were together and had all things in common; they would sell their possessions and goods and distribute them to all, as any had need" (Acts 2:44-45).

Luke's Subversive Christmas Story and True Peace

Pax Romana vs. "Peace on Earth"

"In those days a decree went out from Caesar Augustus that all the world should be registered" (2:1). Caesar's purpose for the census was to establish "peace on earth." This Caesar's name was Octavian (27 BC to AD 14). He was the first Roman emperor following Julius Caesar. The centuries of "peace" that followed were sometimes called Pax Octaviana, Pax Augustiana, or just Pax Romana. For the Roman emperor and his governors this meant no disturbances, rebellions, or threats to the Roman power needed to maintain the steady flow of money and goods to Rome from all over the world. *Pax Romana* was enforced by the most powerful military machine the ancient world had ever known. The stone-paved Roman roads—some still in use today—provided access for the military and commerce all over the empire. Business was protected from bandits on land or from pirates at sea. Slave trade continued until almost half the Roman urban population consisted of slaves. Tax money from individuals or goods poured into Rome from all over the world. The Romans made no attempt to build up local economies unless this meant more revenue for Rome.

Roman soldiers quickly squelched any dissension in order to maintain "peace and security." Dissenters were often punished by speedy punishment without a hearing. Few second chances were ever given. There was no popular voting, opportunity for discussion, and certainly little organized opposition to the invincible Roman armies. This meant that any opposition was only possible by bands of freedom fighters or "terrorists" who had to rely on robbery and extortion to support themselves. These "robbers" were generally a minority feared by the general populace. Romans made use of this atmosphere of fear by posing as saviors keeping people from chaos by promoting Roman law, order, and security.

Caesar, the "Divine Peacemaker"

Caesar claimed divine authority for his role as peacemaker. The Senate honored Octavian with the title of "Augustus" meaning "venerable" or worthy of worship. The Gospel story of tribute to Caesar (Mark 12:13–17) centers on the coin of tribute with its image of the later Tiberius Caesar. The emperor has a divine aura around his head, and the coin reads, "Tiberius Caesar, son of the divine Augustus." Octavian was the first Caesar after Julius. Julius was deified by the Senate only a few months after his death in 42 BC. The Senate gave the same honors to most other emperors, some even in their own lifetime. Octavian erected an altar of peace *(ara pacis)* in the Roman forum, where he and the priests offered sacrifices and prayers for "peace." Later, Octavian and most other emperors were appointed as *pontifex maximus*, supreme high priest, over Roman religion. In this way, Roman emperors posed as divine warriors and peacemakers promoting a holy war against all "evildoers," opposition movements, and terrorists.

Luke's Contrary Peace in the Story of Jesus' Birth

Luke's central purpose is to proclaim Jesus' mission to establish a real inner peace from God rather than the pseudopeace of Pax Romana. This inner peace results from God's hidden plan that Luke outlines in his introductory Gospel dedication to a certain "Theophilus." Luke states his intention to describe "the events fulfilled among us" (1:1). This fulfillment refers to the hidden plan of God that Luke plans to reveal in his Gospel. This divine plan counteracts the external plan of government authorities. Luke will demonstrate how this hidden plan is the "power of the Holy Spirit" behind human events rather than the power of earthly military prowess. We will illustrate this contrast in the following sections.

The Census of the Whole World in Contrast to the Power of a Child

On the outer human side, Caesar Augustus sends out a decree—*dogma*—to register the whole world to establish his absolute control. In the Roman world there was nothing as powerful as a *dogma* from the emperor. But in the divine inner plan, God foils Caesar by making that decree an instrument to fulfill the prophecy that a great ruler will come from Bethlehem: "From you [Bethlehem] shall come forth for me one who is to rule in Israel" (Mic 5:2). Matthew refers to this prophecy explicitly as the Magi come to Jerusalem and ask, "Where is the newly born king of the Jews?" (2:4). In reply, the Magi are directed to Bethlehem according to the prophecy of Micah.

To enforce the Pax Romana, tax money and military conscription were urgently needed. The registration of each person was a necessary means to this end. The main Roman taxes were an individual poll tax and additional taxes on land, produce, and business. In protest of such censuses, there were frequent bitter tax revolts. The Acts of the Apostles mentions one of these under Judas the Galilean around the time of Jesus' birth (5:37). The Roman military thoroughly defeated this uprising, punishing thousands of the Jewish freedom fighters with crucifixion, the cruelest and most shameful execution in the ancient world. Under this atmosphere of terror, Joseph and his expectant wife, Mary, made the long, arduous journey from Nazareth to Bethlehem for registration.

In opposition to Caesar's grandiose plans, God works in a humble way through little ones. Mary gives birth to her firstborn child and lays him in a manger because there is no room for them at the inn (2:7). The divine child is the exemplar for every child of God, as a "little one." The animals in their makeshift shelter provide hospitality. The only welcome committee is composed of shepherds who had been watching over their flocks nearby. In Jesus' own language, a little child was often called a "lamb," *talitha* in Aramaic, as Jesus calls the little girl he raised from the dead in Mark 5:41. So together, animals, shepherds, and children form the ranks of "little ones" to whom Jesus gives the greatest attention. These little ones in turn will give individual attention to others.

The end of Luke's Gospel balances the beginning. Joseph, Mary, and the child find "no room at the inn" at Bethlehem. At the end of the Gospel, two disciples on Easter Sunday were walking to Emmaus when a stranger met them and began to explain Jesus' death in terms of the scriptures. On reaching Emmaus, the stranger acted as if he were continuing going on. However, the disciples "strongly urged him" to stay with them in their lodging. "So he went in and stayed with them" (24:29). As a result, at supper time, the disciples' eyes were opened and they recognized Jesus in the breaking of the bread (24:30–31). In this way, the individual attention and concern for each human person was the direct opposite of the Roman concern for power over the masses in world enrollment through a census. Jesus closes the Gospel with the announcement that "repentance and forgiveness of sins is to be proclaimed in his name to *all peoples of the world*" (24:47). The good news is meant for everyone without exception.

The Child with God's Heavenly Armies in Contrast to Roman Legions

In the darkness of night, a great light indicating the divine presence shone around the shepherds: "The Glory of the *Lord* shone around them" (2:9). This is in contrast to the dim glow (if any!) of the "divine halo" around Caesar's head on Roman coins. The angel announced to the shepherds, "I bring you good news of great joy for all the people: to you is born today in the city of David a Savior, who is the Messiah, the Lord." This title, "Messiah" *(Christos)*, announced the fulfillment of Israel's expectations, but meant little to Romans—except as a possible threat.

However, the titles of Lord, *Kyrios*, and Savior, *Sōtēr*, were quite distinct. Caesar acted as a savior and protector of the world. *Kyrios*, especially in the East, was a title for the gods of the universe and was assumed by many Roman emperors. In contrast, the angels announce that the divine child bears this title, attributed to God in the previous verse, as the glory of the *Lord* shines on the shepherds. In this Gospel, more than any other, Jesus is named as *Lord*. The Acts of the Apostles begins with Pentecost and Peter's proclamation that the prophecy has been fulfilled: "Everyone who calls on the name of the *Lord* shall be saved" (2:21). This becomes a theme in the Acts of the Apostles where the title "Lord" is found over a hundred times. To demonstrate the power of these names, "Suddenly there was with the angel a multitude of the heavenly host." The word *host* translates a military term, *stratia*, an army. In the divine plan, all of Caesar's power and armies are no match for God's power and his heavenly militia.

Jesus' Inner Peace on Earth in Contrast

Before the onset of Jesus' public ministry, the devil tempted him to exercise external power: "Then the devil led him up and showed him in an instant all the kingdoms of the world" (4:4). The "world" is the same word in Greek, *oikoumenē*, found in the story of Jesus' birth where Caesar had decreed that the *whole world* should be registered for purposes of taxation and military control. Jesus rejects the devil's temptation as the direct opposite of God's worship. He answers, "Worship the Lord your God and serve him only." Service and worship of God, with its message of interior peace on earth, is the direct opposite to earthly power used to force people into compliance.

The Child Messiah of Peace Foretold in Scripture

The announcement "Peace on Earth" heralds Jesus' mission as a Messiah of Peace according to the scriptures. We have seen that Luke opened his Gospel by stating that he intended to present "an orderly account of the events that have been fulfilled among us" (1:1). He would expect his audience to know these scriptures as part of Isaiah, the first prophet he mentions by name (3:4). The most important prophecies are those predicting the birth of a future messianic descendant of David. Isaiah, in God's name, declared: "The people who walked in darkness have seen a great light: those who lived in a land of deep darkness—on them light has shined. You have multiplied the nation, you have increased its joy" (9:2–3). This is because

> A *child* has been born for us, *a son* given to us; authority rests upon his shoulders; and he is named Wonderful Counselor, Mighty God, Everlasting Father, *Prince of*

Peace. His authority shall grow continually, and there shall be *endless peace* for the throne of *David* and his kingdom. He will establish and uphold it with justice and righteousness from this time onward and forevermore. The zeal of the LORD *of hosts* will do this. (9:6–7)

The italicized words above are those connected to the Christmas story. Luke explains the meaning of Jesus' birth according to God's plan in the scriptures. Jesus' birth is in Bethlehem, city of *David.* It takes place in *darkness* as shepherds watch over their flocks by night (2:8). The night is suddenly illumined as the "glory of the Lord shone around them" (2:9). As in Isaiah, a joyful atmosphere pervades the birth of Jesus. The angel announces, "I am bringing you good news of great joy for all the people." This is because of the birth of an unusual son, as Mary's time arrives to give birth to a son: "She gave birth to her firstborn *son*" (2:6–7).

The Child King David and the Child Jesus

Also as a child, Jesus' ancestor David was secretly chosen and anointed to be king. God instructed Samuel the prophet, "Go fill your horn with oil and set out; I will send you to Jesse the Bethlehemite, for I have promised for myself a king among his sons" (1 Sam 16:1). On Samuel's arrival in Bethlehem, the city elders were "trembling." They feared that King Saul would hear the news and consider it a threat to his own kingship. They asked Samuel if his coming was (literally) in peace. Samuel replied, "[In] peace." Jesse, David's father, prepared a great welcoming banquet for Samuel. Jesse's seven oldest sons were at table. After noting the strong appearance of the oldest son, Eliab, Samuel thought, "Surely the Lord's anointed [literally, the Messiah of the Lord, in the Greek text, the *Christos*] is now before the LORD" (16:6). However, Samuel heard God's voice tell him not to consider appearances, because "The LORD looks on the heart."

This happened six times as Samuel went down the line to the other six sons, and Samuel said to Jesse, "The LORD has not chosen any of these." Samuel was puzzled and asked Jesse, "Are all your sons here?" Jesse replied, "There remains yet the youngest, but he is keeping sheep." The Greek text of the Bible used by Luke translates "youngest" as *mikros*, "the little one." Children often had the task of tending sheep. David was surely "the least." He was not even invited to the banquet. Then Samuel told Jesse, "Send and bring him; for we will not sit down till he comes here." During the meal, God said to Samuel, "Rise and anoint him, for this is the one." "Then Samuel took the horn of oil and anointed him in the presence of his brothers; and the spirit of the LORD came mightily upon David from that day forward" (16:13).

By comparing this account to Luke's Gospel story, we can see how he used David's story to explain the meaning of Jesus' birth. Luke names David five times (to Mary, 1:27, 32, by Zechariah, 1:69, at Jesus' birth, 2:4, 11). Bethlehem is mentioned twice (2:4, 15). Like Samuel's coming for the anointing, the purpose of the child Jesus is peace on earth, not the deposition of King Herod or Caesar. Samuel does not find David at a regal banquet but in a rustic setting as a child among shepherds, other little ones. The shepherds are mentioned three times in 2:8, 15, 18. Jesse told Samuel that his youngest one was out keeping the sheep. This occupation is again recalled four times in 1 Sam 16:19; 17:15, 28, 34. At Jesus' birth the angel announces to the shepherds that the child is the Messiah (Christ) the Lord. Similarly, Samuel came to Jesse's house to find the anointed (Messiah or Christ) of the Lord (16:6).

Returning to the story of Jesus' birth, we can better perceive the hidden inner conflict. We find on one side Caesar and the Roman Empire, with King Herod their puppet. Luke carefully notes their names (1:5; 2:1). King Herod chose Bethlehem as one of his great military centers. His huge fortress and palace called Herodium was in plain view near Bethlehem. Any census time was particularly dangerous, since fierce tax revolts often sprung up. Many of Herod's soldiers along with Roman troops would have been present in Bethlehem to maintain order. On the other side, a seemingly helpless little child is born. However, God's invisible army, a multitude of the heavenly host, is more powerful than any earthly force or army.

The Sermon on the Plain: A Blueprint and Guide for Peace, Love, and Nonviolence

The Motivation Behind Jesus' Teaching

In Matthew, we studied Jesus' Sermon of the Mount. Jesus was seated on a mountaintop like Moses, who received the Ten Commandments from God. In Luke, Jesus comes down from the mount to a level plain to speak directly to his disciples and a large audience for every time and place. Therefore, we call it "The Sermon on the Plain." Luke's version is much shorter, omitting all references to the scriptures so this summary of Jesus' teachings can reach everyone in the world. Luke wants to show his Gospel audience that Jesus' teaching provides a way his disciples can be always recognized as practicing virtues superior to those much esteemed in the Greek world.

The preparation for this sermon illustrates the central place it holds in this Gospel. Luke has previously described the conflicts between Jesus and religious leaders over the meaning of the Sabbath. In these, Jesus emphasized sensitivity to human need over the letter of the Sabbath-rest laws. Finally, the authorities "were filled with fury and discussed with one another what they might do to Jesus" (6:11). With this foreshadowing of his death, Jesus looks to the future and the continuation of his mission through his teaching and disciples. As a result, he withdrew to pray all night on a mountain before choosing his twelve apostles as special successors (6:12). At dawn, Jesus called his disciples and selected the twelve names Luke records. Then Jesus came down with them to the level plain. There a large crowd from faraway places joined with the disciples to listen to Jesus' instruction. Consequently, Luke's Sermon on the Plain is a special teaching testament that Jesus wishes to hand down to his disciples and the world.

The Sermon Core: Imitation of God

The summit of Jewish piety was imitation of God. This *Imitatio Dei* later became the focus of Christian spirituality. So the center of Jesus' instruction lies in his words, "Be merciful as your

Father is merciful" (6:36). This mercy is God's supreme attribute that he revealed to Moses (Exod 34:6). For "merciful" in the above quotation, Luke has the plural of the Greek *oiktirmōn*. This verbal noun describes the inner felt quality of mercy. Only Luke's Gospel has this word in this place. It is the same word used in the Greek Septuagint Bible as a translation of *rachum* in the revelation of the meaning of God's attributes in Exodus 34:6 and 33:17.

The Inner Roots of Peace: God's "Womb Compassion"

We have already seen in Matthew that this is the motivating force behind identification with others, a key theme in that Gospel. Now we must follow how Luke has also taken this compassion as lying behind the Sermon on the Plains theme of imitation of God. So we will come back with more detail on God's revelation of this quality as the root motive for renewing his covenant of peace with his people. Through the burning bush near Mount Sinai, God revealed his name YHWH to Moses (Exod 3:14). However, gradually in the course of centuries, this sacred name was rarely pronounced out of fear and reverence. Instead, a substitute, *Adonai*, "Lord," was read aloud instead whenever the divine name appeared in the text. The English Bible has LORD, usually in capital and small capital letters to signify this. This name appears some six thousand times. Under this name, God led his people out of Egypt, across the Red Sea, and to Mount Sinai. There Moses climbed the mountain to receive from God the covenant tablets with the Ten Commandments written on them. But when Moses came down from the mountain he found that the people had become impatient for his return and were worshiping the image of a golden calf. In anger, Moses broke the stone tablets and punished those responsible. Then God told Moses he would no longer guide his people to the Promised Land but would send an angel instead.

However, God's apparent refusal was only meant to push Moses to appeal to the forgiving merciful attributes of YHWH. In reply, God promised him he would pass by and reveal the meaning of his name while Moses hid nearby in a rock cleft. Accordingly, the Lord descended and passed by Moses proclaiming, "The LORD (Yahweh), the LORD (Yahweh), a God merciful and gracious, slow to anger and abounding in steadfast love and faithfulness...forgiving iniquity and transgression and sin" (Exod 34:6). The word *merciful* is *rachum* in Hebrew, from the root *rechem*, womb. This primary feminine quality is a deep-felt womb-compassionate love bringing forgiveness, even when the covenant tablets had been disregarded and destroyed. As a result, God agreed to renew his covenant of peace and once again accompany his people to the Promised Land.

In the above text, the first and greatest description of Yahweh's name is the word *rachum*, "merciful." Its meaning lies rooted in a mother's womb. The Bible describes the womb as the location for the beginnings of love. This is where a mother feels the deepest human love: that for her child. Likewise, a child's first experience of love begins in the womb as it perceives a mother's nourishing care poured out from her heart through the throbbing umbilical chord. This is the distinctly feminine aspect of Yahweh's loving nature. The Hebrew noun *rachum* occurs fifty-seven times in the scriptures and the verb around fifty times as the primary attribute of God's nature. Human beings first experience this in the womb where God begins his creative work in such a miraculous manner. Luke's concern about this is mirrored in the fact that he mentions the womb six times in his Gospel as compared to only twice in the rest of the New Testament. Only Luke has the words addressed to Jesus, "Blessed is the womb that bore you and the breasts that nursed you" (11:27).

In the Sermon on the Plain, we have seen above that Luke has the word *merciful*, writing, "Be merciful just as your Father is merciful" (6:36). The Father's "mercy" goes back to the inner *rachum* or womb-compassion that we have just described. Luke describes this using the root meaning of the inner "gut feelings." We have already seen this in the Gospel beginning in Zechariah's Benedictus. There he described the roots of forgiveness coming from the *splangchna* of God like the warmth and light of the rising sun (1:77–79). This *splangchna*, or inner compassion, in Luke becomes the underlying motive behind Jesus' action and the roots of love and nonviolence in the Sermon on the Plain. So first we need to look at some examples of this *splangchna* in Luke's Gospel.

Jesus Acts Like God Through His Mercy

Only Luke has the story of Jesus' visit to Nain and the raising of the only son of a widow (7:11–17). When Jesus and his disciples came near the town gate, they met a departing procession
caused by the greatest tragedy that can face a human being: the
death of the only son of a widow. As Jesus neared the funeral procession, according to custom, he would be expected to join them
and walk with them to the cemetery. Instead, he takes in deeply
the whole pathos. Jesus looked at the widow and felt what she was
going through. He was moved with compassion, *esplangchnisthē*.
Then he ordered the procession of death to stop and he touched
the pall—which would ordinarily bring upon him the ritual impu-
rity of death. Instead, his touch brought new life as the young man
sat up and began to talk. With a gesture of kindness, Jesus
restored him to his mother. The crowd at Nain was overcome
with awe and exclaimed, "A great prophet has risen among us"
and "God has visited his people" (7:16).

We note in the above story that Jesus took the initiative.
Also, this was not something just planned in his mind. He allowed
himself to be moved and take in all the sorrow and grief that was
going on. His action flowed freely from this "passivity," which was
like that of God when he first came to Moses at the burning bush
at Sinai. God said to Moses, "I have observed the misery of my
people who are in Egypt; I have heard their cry on account of
their taskmasters. Indeed, I know their sufferings, and I have
come down to deliver them from the Egyptians" (Exod 3:7). The
sequence of the expressions, *observe*, *hear*, and *know*, followed by
the response, is moving and significant. These expressions show
that God's action follows the opening of himself to the misery and
suffering of his people.

The parable of the Good Samaritan is only in Luke and parallels Jesus' own loving initiative and open response to need. An
unknown stranger was traveling down the winding, dangerous
road from Jerusalem to Jericho. A band of robbers ambushed him
around a road bend. "They stripped him, beat him, and went
away, leaving him half dead" (10:31). A priest and then a Levite
soon came down the road. In each case they saw the victim from

some distance but took care not to get too near by deliberately passing by on the other side of the road. Some time later a traveling Samaritan, regarded as a foreigner, came along and risked coming near the unfortunate victim. As a result, he was moved with compassion, *esplangchnisthē*. This prompted him to take every possible means to help, even at risk to himself. At the end of the parable, Jesus' advice to the Gospel audience is "Go and do likewise" (10:37). Here the divine *splangchna* or mercy works even through someone traditionally regarded as an enemy. Again we note that the Samaritan did not just pass by, but opened himself to the situation. He came near, saw, and completely responded in every possible way, even at risk to himself. In contrast, the priest and Levite, who were official teachers, deliberately "passed by the other side" so they would not be moved emotionally or involved.

Again only in Luke, the parable of the prodigal son applies the same theme of forgiveness. A young son demanded his share of his parents' inheritance and went off to a foreign country where he squandered everything. He was finally reduced to the most shameful occupation for a Jew: that of feeding pigs for Gentile owners. Finally, he woke up to what had happened to his life, remembered his parents' love, and decided to return home. His father (representing God) also was thinking of him at the same time. Every day he watched the road for some sign of his son in the distance. One day he spotted the boy afar off and was moved with compassion, *esplangchnisthē*.

This deep inner feeling prompted the father to run "foolishly" to his son, put his arms around him, and kiss him. Not only that, he even arranged the greatest party ever seen in those parts. He brought new clothes for his son, hired an orchestra with dancers, and prepared a sumptuous meal. The fatted calf (mentioned four times), reserved for extraordinary occasions, was brought out and roasted. The attitude of the elder son on seeing all this represents those of the Gospel audience who might think, "What about us who have always been faithful?" The father can only reply, "Son, you are always with me and all that is mine is yours. But we had to celebrate and rejoice, because this brother of yours was dead and has come to life; he was lost and has been found" (15:32).

In each case above, we notice that God or human beings are moved by first paying sensitive, careful attention. At Nain, the text literally reads that "seeing her, the Lord was moved to compassion" (7:13). In the Good Samaritan parable, there is a sharp contrast: Both the priest and Levite did not want to come close to the wounded man to absorb the full impact of what had happened, but passed deliberately on the other side of the road. However the Samaritan came near him and was deeply moved (10:33). The father of the prodigal son watched the road ready to be moved by his son's need (15:20). Consequently, love does not flow from an act of the will, but from deliberately leaving one's self open and vulnerable to the need of others.

The Sermon on the Plain: Praxis of Peace, Nonviolence, and Love for Enemies

"Love your enemies, do good to those who hate you, bless those who curse you, pray for those who abuse [persecute] you" (6:27). Matthew's Sermon on the Mount asks for prayer for persecutors (5:44), but Luke's version takes a giant step further. Jesus asks for specific good actions toward enemies. Thus there is no hint of passive acceptance or resignation: It is active response to evil and evildoers in a surprising way. Jesus' teaching mirrors his own actions. Even on the cross he prays for those who are torturing and killing him (24:34). At the Last Supper, Jesus prays for Simon Peter because he knows he will give in to human weakness and betray him (22:31). Jesus even takes the initiative to turn and look at Peter after his betrayal as an invitation to reconciliation. Even to Judas, Jesus extends hope by asking him at his arrest, "Is it with a kiss that you are betraying the Son of Man?" (22:47). As a practical application of "doing good to enemies," Jesus even healed the ear of an attacker who was injured at his arrest by one of his disciples (22:51).

"Bless those who curse you." A curse was an effective way of hurting others by invoking the worst punishments of God. The ancient world was very much afraid of "bad vibrations" of this kind. To reverse this by a kind blessing would be a great surprise. This was not just an ideal but actually put in practice by traveling apostles. St. Paul described to the Corinthians how he responded to such curses: "When reviled we bless; when persecuted we endure; when slandered we speak kindly" (1 Cor 4:12–13).

"Pray for those who persecute you." The people most in our thoughts are both those whom we love and those who hurt us. So this is an automatic reminder to pray even for those who invade our minds.

> If anyone strikes you on the cheek, offer the other also; and from anyone who takes away your coat do not withhold even your shirt. Give to everyone who begs from you; and if anyone takes away your goods, do not ask for them again. (6:29–30)

"Turning the other cheek" has become over the centuries a hyperbolic expression for preferring even a second injury to responding with violence. A strike on the face or cheek was a shameful insult in ancient times that would usually lead to prompt retaliation to preserve a sense of honor. A coat or cloak was the outer garment that could be taken away either by theft or as a loan security. But the shirt or tunic was immediately over the skin, so taking it away would leave someone completely naked. This is really a humorous exaggeration, giving an added gift to someone violently taking one's clothes away. Importunate beggars following people around to shame them into giving would ordinarily prompt an angry dismissal. Instead, they are to be treated with generous and cheerful giving. This transforms what is practically a robbery into a loving gift. The whole theme of these sayings is that of overcoming evil with cheerful good actions.

"Do to others as you would have them do to you" (6:31) is a summary we have seen in Matthew as the Golden Rule. However, the expression does not regard self-love as a criterion but views the self as the cherished image of God at creation (Gen 1:26). This summary is so important that Luke repeats it when a lawyer asks Jesus what must be done to gain eternal life. Jesus responds with the traditional *Shema* (Hear!) about loving God with one's whole heart, soul, mind, and heart (10:27). Luke does not add "you shall love your neighbor as yourself" as a second commandment, but joins it to the Shema so there is but one single commandment. This means that love of God and love of human beings are one and the same. This is illustrated by the parable of the Good Samaritan that follows in Luke's Gospel.

The next section in the sermon is meant to be a sharp contrast to the Greek ideal of friendship that for many had the characteristics of a good investment. Reciprocity, mutual loans, and advantageous business partnerships were hoped-for outcomes:

> "If you love those who love you, what credit is that to you? For even sinners love those who love them. If you do good to those who do good to you, what credit is that to you? For even sinners do the same. If you lend to those from whom you hope to receive, what credit is that to you? Even sinners lend to sinners, to receive as much again." (6:32–4)

Luke is anxious to show that Jesus' teaching goes far beyond Greek virtues. Real love must reach out to all without ulterior motivation and without expectations of payoffs or gratitude.

> But love your enemies, do good, and lend, expecting nothing in return. Your reward will be great, and you will be children of the Most High; for he is kind to the ungrateful and the wicked. Be merciful, just as your Father is merciful. (6:35–36)

Love of enemies is repeated again as the distinct quality of the love Jesus teaches. This receives a special reward from God because it makes a person like God in the quality of that love. This is especially true of mercy, which we have seen as the supreme quality of God's *rachum*. The subject of forgiving debts will come up again in the Lord's Prayer (11:4). To make sure that forgiveness of debts would not impede lending, Luke brings out the importance of lending even with limited or no hope of return.

Judgments and Disparagement of Others

Luke gives more space and emphasis to this area than Matthew. In a culture that is predominantly oral and not written, words and the attitudes expressed by them have much more power and are communicated more widely. Thus they have an even larger responsibility for creating enemies and setting up barriers to peace, reconciliation, and friendship.

> "Do not judge, and you will not be judged; do not condemn, and you will not be condemned. Forgive, and you will be forgiven; give, and it will be given to you. A good measure, pressed down, shaken together, running over, will be put into your lap; for the measure you give will be the measure you get back." (6:37–38)

In the above text, "judging" and "condemning" are parallel and almost the same. They include derogatory remarks about others, finding fault, put-downs, carping, and the like. The contrast, "You will be judged or forgiven," omits God's name because of the common habit of avoiding it; so it is God who really judges. The words expressed by people about others often reveal more about themselves than others, and thus God will judge accordingly. On the positive side, a forgiving attitude shows the right disposition to being forgiven by God. However, this is not just tit-for-tat. God's forgiveness and true peace go far beyond human practices. Thus it is unlike the prevalent way of measuring grain at that time. The ordinary seller does not pack the grain down or fill it to an overflowing brim, but does just the opposite in giving the minimum.

Luke then has Jesus apply this to teachers, who too often go beyond bounds in correcting others, rather than relying on example. Jesus declares in a parable, "Can a blind person guide a blind person? Will not both fall into a pit? A disciple is not above the teacher, but everyone who is fully qualified will be like the teacher" (6:3).

Concentration on changing others rather than one's self can result in treating them as objects, not people. Likewise, it makes teachers fail to see their own faults. So Jesus says,

"Why do you see the speck in your neighbor's eye, but do not notice the log in your own eye? Or how can you say to your neighbor, 'Friend, let me take out the speck in your eye,' when you yourself do not see the log in your own eye? You hypocrite, first take the log out of your own eye, and then you will see clearly to take the speck out of your neighbor's eye." (6:41–42)

Jesus and teachers in the early church taught in a personal manner, dealing with individuals and small groups. They regarded the contagion of good example as the best way to inculcate virtue. Luke reinforces this by having Jesus give examples of a tree and its fruit and the contrast of a grapevine that produces thorns. Using Luke's favorite image of the heart, Jesus points out that meaningful words come from the "good treasure of the heart" (6:45). In Luke, Jesus concludes by adding, "Why do you call me 'Lord, Lord,' and do not do what I tell you?" "Lord, Lord" was a repeated invocation of prayer. Yet even this means little if it does not emerge from the treasury of the heart that is open to Jesus' word and puts it into practice.

Jesus, Messiah of Peace and Nonviolence in the Passion Story

Luke has planned the passion narrative so his audience will understand their own role as followers of Jesus and as peacemakers. We keep in mind that Luke was writing near the end of the first century. Jerusalem had finally succumbed to Rome in AD 70 after a long war that ended with the Temple's destruction. However, the violent resistance to Rome still continued in Luke's time and later led to another revolution in AD 132–35 under Bar Kochba. This leader was able to restore the Temple sacrifices for a brief period.

Jesus' Triumphant Entry into Jerusalem and Final Teachings on Peace

At the end of his journey to Jerusalem, Jesus approached the Mount of Olives and prepared for his important entry into the capital. Luke describes this as a precelebration of all that was to happen because of Jesus' message of peace. First there is a detailed instruction about requisitioning a donkey for Jesus' entry. As Jesus rode into the city, his disciples spread out their garments to form a "red carpet" before him. The detailed plans and descriptions point to a scriptural sign. The prophet Zechariah had written: "Rejoice greatly, O daughter Zion! Shout aloud, O daughter Jerusalem! Lo, your king comes to you; triumphant and victorious is he, humble and riding on a donkey.... He will cut off the chariot from Ephraim and the war horse from Jerusalem…and he shall command peace to the nations" (9:9–10).

The donkey, the joyful shouting, the mention of the king, and the purpose of peace all link together. Jesus does not ride on a triumphant white horse but a humble donkey. His purpose is to do away with military chariots and war horses in order to bring a message of peace. A multitude of disciples praised God, saying, "Blessed is the king who comes in the name of the Lord! Peace in heaven, and glory in highest heaven" (19:38). Here Luke brings out a striking parallel to the "peace on earth" message at Jesus' birth. The text reads, "Peace in heaven," because Jesus will soon be returning there. "Glory in highest heaven" is the identical praise of the angels at Jesus' birth (2:14). There is a multitude of disciples just as there was a multitude of angels at Jesus' birth. However, Jesus is filled with sorrow as he drew near to Jerusalem:

> As he came near and saw the city, he wept over it saying, "If you, even you, had only recognized on this day the things that make for peace but they are hidden from your eyes. Indeed, the days will come upon you, when your enemies will set up ramparts around you and will surround you, and hem you in on every side. (19:41–43)

Jesus is not describing a generic responsibility of Jerusalem or its people in regard to the war with Rome and the resulting disastrous defeat of its defenders. Josephus's account of this war is one of the most gruesome ever written. Jesus breaks down in tears as he imagines the horrors of that war. The shedding of blood is the greatest obstacle to true shalom. However, only a minority in Israel really wanted war with Rome. It was the determined work of violent revolutionaries under military leaders who proclaimed themselves to be prophets or messiahs and invincible instruments of God. The "time of visitation" is Jesus' coming not as a military leader but as a Messiah of Peace.

Jesus again described the fate of Jerusalem and the Temple in his last discourse. When some remarked to Jesus about the beauty of the Temple and its buildings, he predicted a day when "not one stone will be left upon another; all will be thrown down" (21:6). On being asked what signs would point to this, Jesus replied, "Beware that you are not led astray; for many will come in my name and say 'I am he!' and 'the time is near.' Do not go after them" (21:7). These words of Jesus refer to false leaders proclaiming themselves as messiahs and appealing to people by promising great signs and victories in war like those of Moses in the past. There were many false messiahs in the years before the war with Rome. Even in the second war with Rome from AD 132 to 135, the Jewish leader Bar Kochba declared to the people that he was the Messiah.

In addition, along the same lines Jesus said, "When you hear of wars and insurrections, do not be terrified; for these things must take place first, but the end will not follow immediately" (21:9). Many people believed there would be a final holy war, a great "mother of all wars" against the forces of evil before the end of the world. Yet God would bring victory to his people despite overwhelming odds. The Book of Revelation refers to this type of battle when the "final bowls of God's wrath" were poured out. Demonic spirits, working great signs, assemble all the kings of the earth "for battle on the great day of God almighty" (16:14). They assemble all their forces together "in the place that in Hebrew is called Harmagedon" (16:16) to make war against God's people. Jesus warns against the great deception of leaders who try to convince people they are God's chosen leaders, leading them to triumphant victory over evildoers and God's enemies.

Jesus' Command to Stop Violence During His Arrest

Following the Last Supper, Jesus and his disciples went to Mount Olivet to pray. He knew his mission was to preach the good news of the kingdom in the capital city, yet it was still possible for him to withdraw by night to Galilee where his large following afforded him support and safety. Jesus' love for Jerusalem impelled him to go there, yet he well knew the experience of prophets of peace before him. He had previously said to his disciples, "Jerusalem, Jerusalem, the city that kills the prophets and stones those who are sent to it! How often have I desired to gather your children together as a hen gathers her brood under her wings, and you were not willing!" (13:34).

Jesus' temptation is often called "The Agony in the Garden." However, the Greek word *agonia*, found only here in Luke, means a painful struggle rather than only suffering. Luke's description differs sharply from those in Matthew and Mark. Only in Luke does Jesus' prayer prepare for the disciples' temptation to violently resist Jesus' captors. Therefore, the episode begins and ends with these same words to his disciples, "Pray that you may not come into the time of trial" (22:40). Then Jesus withdrew from them, knelt down on the ground and prayed, "Father, if you are willing, remove this cup from me; yet, not my will but yours be done." When Jesus finished his prayer, the crowd coming to arrest Jesus suddenly appeared on the scene, led by Judas. Jesus stood his ground and let Judas approach him for the kiss of betrayal.

At this moment, the surrounding disciples asked Jesus' permission to make an armed violent defense. They said, "Lord, shall we strike with the sword?" (22:49). However, they did not wait for Jesus' answer. Instead, "One of them struck the slave of the high priest and cut off his right ear." Jesus sharply reprimanded the disciples, "No more of this." Then to show how much this violence of his followers displeased him, "He touched his ear and healed him." Thus Jesus' own response was in healing, forgiving, nonviolence. The attacking crowd was reinforced with Temple police armed with swords and clubs, ready to arrest a violent revolutionary. In contrast, Jesus tells them, "Have you come out with swords and clubs as if I were a bandit?" The translation, "bandit," is of the Greek word, *lēstēs*, which also describes the two "bandits" crucified at the right and left of Jesus in the gospels of Mark and Matthew. It applied to violent revolutionaries who extorted or robbed money from people in order to support their activities. Jesus had no part in such activities. In contrast, he taught openly each day in the Temple. He declares, "When I was with you day after day in the Temple, you did not lay hands on me." As a final statement, Jesus told the attacking mob, "This is your hour and the power of darkness" (23:53).

Luke's Gospel teaches that trust in violent power is a sign of temptation from Satan. Jesus had already warned against this temptation in the garden where he twice asked his disciples to pray that they enter not into temptation. From what follows, this temptation was to use violent power to resist Judas and his band. The whole arrest account in Luke is centered about Jesus' refusal to submit to that temptation. Luke also shows that at every step Jesus freely and voluntarily went ahead. He was not a mere helpless victim of those plotting his death. He would not be a Messiah of Peace by surrender or submission but by deliberate choice. This was meant to be a model for his followers and the Gospel audience.

Jesus as Messiah of Peace in the Trial Before Pilate

Luke writes that the puppet ruling assembly came before Pilate and accused Jesus, "We found this man perverting our nation, forbidding us to pay taxes to the emperor, and saying that he himself is the Messiah, a king" (23:2). The first of these three charges is better explained in 23:5, when the prosecutors insist: "He stirs up the people by teaching through all Judea, from Galilee where he began even to this place." The claims were ones that would immediately draw the attention of any Roman governor. Anyone stirring up people or promoting dissension was an enemy of the Pax Romana that every governor made a priority. Roman taxation was always a primary cause of revolts. Jesus' teaching to "give to the emperor the things that are the emperor's" (20:25) was taken out of the context that it is subordinated to a total service to God: "[Give] to God the things that are God's."

As for the accusation of proclaiming himself to be a king, a Messiah, Jesus never openly proclaimed himself to be one. When

Peter declared that Jesus was the Messiah, Jesus rebuked and silenced him (9:21). In regard to being a king, only the Palm Sunday crowd acclaimed Jesus with this title (19:38). Pilate then directly questioned Jesus: "Are you the king of the Jews?" Jesus answered, "You say so." The "you" is emphatic in Greek to emphasize that the words are Pilate's not Jesus' own. Then Pilate told the chief priests and crowd, "I find no basis for an accusation against this man" (23:4). When Pilate heard that Jesus was from Galilee, he sent him to King Herod, who was also in Jerusalem at this time. Jesus refused to answer Herod's questions. In response, Herod's soldiers mocked Jesus over the whole idea of such a powerless figure being a king compared to Herod. So King Herod sent Jesus back to Pilate as a witness of Jesus' innocence.

Another dramatic presentation of Jesus as a man of peace came when the crowd asked Pilate to release a prisoner according to the Passover custom. They asked for Barabbas, "a man who had been put in prison for an insurrection that had taken place in the city and for murder." Thus Jesus is the very opposite of such a violent revolutionary figure. Pilate then proclaims Jesus' innocence a third time. However, he finally gives in to the crowd assembled by the puppet authorities and hands Jesus over to the soldiers for crucifixion. Luke heightens the contrast by repeating that Barabbas the violent, even murderous prisoner was released at the same time (23:25).

The Cross and the Final Witness of Jesus as Messiah of Peace

On the way to Calvary, a group of women followed Jesus "beating their breasts and wailing for him" (23:27). Jesus turned to them and said, "Daughters of Jerusalem, do not weep for me but for yourselves and for your children" (23:28). These words recall Jesus' previous prediction of horrible destruction of Jerusalem during the war with Rome (21:20–24). He deeply understood how women were the first victims of every war as they witnessed the destruction of their own children. Once again we see the shedding of innocent blood as the greatest obstacle to shalom. The war with Rome was initiated by a minority group that followed military messiahs rather than leaders like Jesus, a Messiah of Peace.

The end of Jesus' life echoes the beginning theme of "peace on earth." Two other men were crucified, one at Jesus' right and one at his left. Matthew and Mark call them "robbers." But they were "robbers" in the sense that they were "freedom fighters" opposed to Roman military occupation. To support their cause they frequently robbed or extorted money from the populace. Today we might call them "terrorists." Luke calls them literally "workers of evil" or "evildoers." For the centurion and his soldiers, Jesus' execution was one more Roman triumph in their "holy war" against terrorists and dissenters threatening the security and peace of a military Pax Romana.

The soldiers mocked Jesus, saying, "If you are the King of the Jews, save yourself" (23:37). Luke notes that "there was also an inscription over him, 'This is the King of the Jews.'" This inscription and the preceding taunt of "King of the Jews" convey to the Gospel audience that Jesus is truly a king through the folly and ignominy of the cross.

At this point, one of the two men crucified with Jesus began to see things quite differently from the taunting crowds, soldiers, and even the other crucified man. He rebuked his companion and declared, "Do you not fear, since we are under the same sentence of condemnation? And we indeed justly for we are getting what we deserve for our deeds, but this man has done no wrong." Then he said, "Jesus, remember me when you come into your kingdom." Jesus replied, "Truly, I tell you, today you will be with me in Paradise" (23:43).

In a dramatic last moment, Jesus forgave even a terrorist at his side by choosing him to be the first to enter heaven in his company. Jesus' concluding words proclaim to a gospel audience of any time that a military Pax Romana was a delusion not only for Rome but for any government following the same path. In contrast, true "peace on earth" comes through love and forgiveness—not through violence, force, and war. Two striking divine signs confirmed Jesus' words: The sun darkened and the Temple veil was torn. These signs heralded the inauguration of the kingdom

Jesus had promised. The Holy of Holies had been the exclusive place for the forgiveness of sins, but now it is open to all.

"Then Jesus, with a loud voice cried out, said, 'Father into your hands I commend my spirit.' Having said this he breathed his last." These last words of Jesus' complete trust in his Father deeply moved the Roman centurion. "He praised God and said, "Certainly this man was innocent [literally, "just"]." This hardened soldier, a specialist in crucifixions of revolutionaries and terrorists, admits he has made a mistake about Jesus. The centurion saw that Jesus died as a Messiah of Peace with peaceful words of forgiveness and acting as head of an unearthly, divine kingdom. Others joined in this recognition as "all the crowds who had gathered for this spectacle saw what had taken place and returned, beating their breasts" (23:48).

The Message of Peace in the Resurrection Appearances

The resurrection account is a necessary completion of the cross. Jesus' innocence along with his resurrection are two concerns linked with the Gospel prelude. There Luke announced the purpose of his Gospel: that readers might know the "truth" (in the sense of "certainty") about the things in which they have been instructed (1:4). First the centurion had declared, "Certainly this man was innocent" (23:47). The identical Greek word for "certainly," *ontōs*, also occurs in the disciples' statement: "The Lord has risen indeed [certainly] and has appeared to Simon (24:34)." This Greek word is only found in Luke in these two verses.

On the women's arrival at Jesus' tomb on Easter Sunday, they did not find Jesus' body. However, two men in dazzling clothes appeared to them and announced, "Why do you look for the living among the dead? He is not here but has risen" (24:5). Then the two mysterious men (or angels) recalled Jesus' words to them, "Remember, how he told you while he was still in Galilee, that the Son of Man *must* be handed over to sinners, and be crucified, and on the third day rise again." The word *must* is italicized because it indicates God's plan in the scriptures that are the source of certainty. This "remembering" is especially evident in the three times that Jesus had predicted his own death and resurrection. However, on each occasion the disciples did not understand because it was the hidden plan of God about the mystery of the cross (9:22, 48; 18:31–34). After this, Luke notes that the women "remembered his words, and returning from the tomb, they told all this to the eleven and to all the rest" (24:8–9).

The second indication of the scriptures as God's plan takes place during the journey of two disciples from Jerusalem to Emmaus on that same day. While they were walking, a traveler joined them who was really the risen Jesus in disguise. He asked them what they had been discussing. In sadness, they replied they were talking about Jesus of Nazareth and how they were deeply disappointed after his condemnation and crucifixion. The stranger then chided them on their slowness to believe in the prophets. "Then beginning with Moses and all the prophets, he interpreted to them the things about himself in all the scriptures" (24:27). The Acts of the Apostles cites many of these scriptures. The most significant is in a parallel situation when Philip the evangelist met a traveling Ethiopian official (8:26–40). This official was returning from Jerusalem in his chariot while reading the following prophecy from Isaiah:

> Like a sheep he was led to the slaughter, and like a lamb silent before its shearer, so he does not open his mouth. In his humiliation justice was denied him. Who can describe his generation? For his life is taken away from the earth. (53:7–8)

In New Testament times, when one passage like this is quoted, the audience is expected to know other verses in the same context. Isaiah describes a dedicated Servant of God, a faithful Israelite in exile who no longer had the consoling support of Temple worship. Despite this loss, he does not lose hope but offers his own life, like a nonviolent lamb as if a Temple sacrifice for his own people and others. As a result, God announces through Isaiah, "The righteous one, my servant, shall make many righteous, and he shall bear their iniquities" (53:11). Also, "He was wounded for our transgressions, crushed for our iniquities; upon him was the punishment that made us whole" (53:5).

These last words in the Hebrew are literally that he (God) "brought his peace," *shalom*, on us. The corresponding Greek translation reads literally that God "laid on him the discipline or teaching of our peace *(eirēnē)*." The evangelist Philip drew near the chariot and offered to explain the scripture to the Ethiopian. Then, "starting with this scripture, he proclaimed to him the good news about Jesus." Philip taught the official that this scripture must be applied to Jesus, who voluntarily gave his life in sacrifice for others as a Messiah of Peace.

After the travelers' arrival in Emmaus, Jesus revealed himself as the mysterious stranger who interpreted the scriptures. After he vanished, the disciples said to one another, "Were not our hearts burning within us, while he was talking to us on the road, while he was opening the scriptures to us?" (24:32). The disciples then immediately returned to Jerusalem, where they found the eleven and others gathered together. While they were talking about what had happened, Jesus suddenly stood among them and greeted them with the words, "Peace be with you." These words carry special energy as Jesus' farewell greeting. They sum up Jesus' own special ministry and personal dedication to peace.

This final greeting of peace prepares the way for a third and final reference to the divine plan in scripture and the disciples' mission to carry Jesus' ministry of peace to the world.

> Then he opened their minds to understand the scriptures, and said to them, "Thus it is written, that the Christ should suffer and on the third day rise from the dead, and that repentance and forgiveness of sins should be preached in his name to all nations, beginning from Jerusalem. You are witnesses of these things. And behold, I send the promise of my Father upon you; but stay in the city, until you are clothed with power from on high." (24:45–49)

In the words above we find a summary of Jesus' peace-centered commission. In his name, the disciples are to be agents of a

Messiah of Peace to bring to the world repentance, *metanoia*, forgiveness of sins, along with an active witness, *martyres*, in their own lives. To enable them to do so, Jesus will send them "the promise of my Father" that will provide them with Jesus' identity and power. "Then he led them as far as Bethany, and lifting up his hands, he blessed them" (24:50). The blessing he pronounced would have been the priestly blessing in Numbers 6:24–26, with its final petition prayer that the Lord "give you peace." Thus "peace," shalom, is the last word spoken by Jesus on earth. This shalom is not just an idea, state, or concept, but an energizing divine energy that Jesus sends to the Gospel audience of any time when they read or listen to Luke's Gospel.

Summary Points for Praxis, Teaching, and Ministry

- Luke's story of Jesus' birth and the announcement of "Peace on Earth" is really subversive in its contrast to Pax Romana. That so-called "peace" was a military solution based on fear so others would comply with Roman plans to dominate world economics for their own greedy interests. In contrast, Jesus' peace is inner, relying on "little ones" who follow Jesus' way not of domination but of humble, loving service.

- Of all the gospels, Luke has the strongest portrait of Jesus as a Messiah of Peace and nonviolence, especially in the passion account. A true follower is a man or woman of peace who follows the guidelines of the Sermon on the Plain with its emphasis on love of enemies, nonviolence, and renunciation of retaliation. The supreme model is imitation of God in the words, "Be merciful as your Father is merciful" (6:36).

- Jesus in Luke also has the greatest focus on repentance, or metanoia. The biblical model for this is prophetic justice. This is distinct from charity or generous giving. Prophetic justice is based on the land and its resources as gifts of God that are lent to human beings so they may be equally shared with others. Since the land and resources of this planet are limited, if any one has overabundance while someone else does not have enough this is evil in itself and must be remedied by forgiveness and definite change, as illustrated in the story of Zaccheus (19:1–9).

• Only in Luke do we find love of God and love of neighbor united in one command (10:27). In Jesus, this love is described using the root *splangkna*, meaning "gut compassion." The same love source as in Jesus can be found in humans, as illustrated by the story of the Good Samaritan. This love is activated by exposure to those who are in need but remains inactive when, like the Hebrew priest and Levite in the story, we detour and "pass by on the other side of the road." In contrast, the Good Samaritan saw and allowed himself to be deeply moved to the extent of loving service and healing to the limit of his means. At the end, Jesus can only give this answer to the lawyer who asked who was his neighbor. The answer directed to him and the Gospel audience is: "Go and do likewise" (10:37).

THE GOSPEL OF JOHN: PAX ROMANA VS. PAX CHRISTI

"Peace I leave with you; my peace I give to you." (John 14:27)

The Situation of the Gospel Community

Outside of this Gospel itself, there is little certain information about where or when it was written. So we must turn to the text itself to give us some idea of the community's concerns. It is easy to discover a strong atmosphere of fear in the background. The first type is the fear of punishment from Jewish authorities. At the feast of Tabernacles, people were afraid to speak openly about Jesus because of "fear of the Jews" (7:13). (By "Jews" is usually meant the Judean authorities under Rome.) In the story of the man born blind, his parents would not speak for the same reason "for the Jews had already agreed that anyone who confessed Jesus to be Messiah would be put out of the synagogue" (9:22). Finally, the cured blind man was himself actually thrown out (9:34)

Among the government authorities themselves, some did believe in Jesus but were afraid to confess this lest they be put out of the synagogue (12:42). At Jesus' burial, Joseph of Arimathea was a secret disciple of Jesus because of the same fear. The description of Nicodemus as having come to Jesus at night is also an indicator of this fear (3:1; 19:39). In his last discourse, Jesus warns his disciples that they will be cast out of the synagogues

(16:2). To be outlawed from the synagogue was a very serious matter. It was often like a living death because people became separated from the vital centers of religion, culture, and society. The author describes the early disciples as gathered together behind locked doors on the evening of Jesus' resurrection because of the fear of Jewish authorities (20:19, 26).

However, this first type of fear was small in comparison to that of the Roman military authority. There was little independent Jewish authority in the first century. King Herod in Galilee was a puppet king, and Judea was under a Roman governor, who appointed the high priest each year. The high priest and elders formed a Sanhedrin to rule the people under the watchful eye of Rome. The greatest Roman concern was the appearance of any leaders whom the people could look up to as messiahs or liberators of their people. So Jewish authorities were anxious to denounce to Rome any such men. As has happened through history, they made use of informers like Judas to secretly look for and denounce possible dissenters or instigators.

The trial of Jesus before Pilate was typical of what many Christians must have faced if they were denounced as followers of a leader who claimed to be a messiah or king. The questions to Jesus as to whether he was king of the Jews are indicative. The crowd pressed Pilate, "If you release this man, you are no friend of the emperor. Everyone who claims to be a king sets himself against the emperor" (19:12). The profession of the chief priests, "We have no king but Caesar" (19:15), is one that every subject of the empire was expected to make if pressed to do so. Pilate's surrender to fear despite his convictions is a warning to the Gospel audience not to follow the same path. The divinization of Caesar in the Roman Empire at this time is the very opposite of the climactic confession of Thomas, "My Lord and my God" (20:28). *Kyrios* (Lord) and *theos* (god) were divine titles claimed by various Roman emperors. In his last discourse, Jesus had said, "They will put you out of the synagogues. Indeed, an hour is coming when those who kill you will think that by doing so they are offering worship to God" (16:2).

The Cross as Key to the Gospel

Unlike the others, John's Gospel begins with a prologue, yet it is really a summary that presupposes a reading of the whole Gospel. The entire Gospel not only ends with the cross, but centers around its meaning. The Gospel audience already knew about the cross, yet the writer intends to lead them deeper into its meaning from the fruit of his own contemplation. So he pictures himself as Jesus' beloved disciple standing at the foot of the cross looking on all that is happening. He writes that Jesus on the cross "saw his mother and the disciple whom he loved standing beside her" (19:26). The last words of the description of Jesus' death are a quotation from scripture, "They will look upon the one whom they have pierced" (Zech 12:10). So the writer is among those who "look on the cross" and find a deeper meaning to share with the Gospel audience.

In-depth Seeing "Your King"

The way of sharing this insight about the cross is through a series of references to seeing (some eight times) so the audience can also see in a deeper way. This seeing will focus on the title of King or King of the Jews and will gradually move to a final image of Jesus as king of peace for all the world. The first scene began when the soldiers flogged Jesus and then wove a crown of thorns, put it on his head, and dressed him in a purple robe. This is a frightful contrast, for his whole body was like one large bleeding wound. The Roman floggings were long and unmerciful. The purpose was to greatly weaken prisoners so they could not survive much longer on the cross. After his flogging, Jesus was dressed as a king with a crown and royal robes.

Following this, the soldiers took turns coming up to Jesus, bowing in feigned reverence, and saluting him as if he were the emperor, saying, "Hail, King of the Jews." Then they would suddenly slap him on the face and laugh. Such a blow was an extreme form of humiliation. The *"Ave Rex"* insult is a play on Caesar's special greeting of honor. These shameful insults were actually more hurtful than the cross, for they directly debased Jesus' personal honor in front of everyone. "King of the Jews" is repeated six times in this Gospel, more than in any other gospel, and becomes an insulting title. For the audience, "look" or "behold" are repeated three times, inviting a search for deeper meaning.

In this first "look" scene, Pilate went out to the people and told them, "Look, I am bringing him out to you to let you know that I find no case against him" (19:4). Then Jesus came out wearing the crown of thorns and purple robe. Only John's Gospel mentions the crown of thorns and purple robe a second time for the greatest possible emphasis. Then Pilate has the second "look" scene as he says to the people, "Here is the man," literally, "Look," or "behold," the man. The chief priests and their police only replied by repeatedly shouting, "Crucify him! Crucify him."

In all these events, there is a hidden level of divine power at work. This is shown in the next incident inside the praetorium where Pilate orders Jesus to answer him, saying, "Do you not know that I have power to release you, and power to crucify you?" Jesus responds, "You would have no power over me unless it had been given to you from above." In other words, Pilate is unknowingly acting as God's agent, making it possible for the audience to really look in a deeper way at what is happening. Jesus' shame becomes his glory as God acts through the ultimate disgrace of the cross.

Because of this reversal theme, this Gospel is the most "glorious," with the noun or verb occurring more than the other gospels together. Jesus' shame becomes his glory. At the Last Supper, after Judas' departure to betray him, Jesus says, "Now the Son of Man has been glorified." In his final prayer, in chapter 17, Jesus notes this glory seven times. The audience's challenge is to love God's glory more than human glory (12:43). In contrast, Pilate's "glory" is at stake. Jesus' opponents cry out to the governor, "If you release this man, you are no friend of the emperor" (19:12). The "friends of the emperor" were bearers of that special title and comprised an elite group around Caesar with special honor and privileges. Pilate, if he was a faithful governor with good recommendations, would aspire to this honor. So now Jesus' opponents hint they could provide an unfavorable report to Rome.

The Judgment of Caesar
and the Judgment of God

The judgment of Pilate, as of Caesar, is supreme in the Roman world. He sits on Caesar's bema, or judgment seat, as the Acts of the Apostles notes (26:10). The judgment seat is "at a place called *Lithostratos*," or Stone Pavement, another Roman note only here in John (19:13). But while Pilate appears to be the judging power, it is really God who is judging the world. The text notes that it is about noon, the time when the Passover lambs were being prepared for the evening sacrifice. God's plan makes Pilate an instrument in making Jesus the new Passover sacrifice. This judgment reversal appears several times in the Gospel.

Referring to his death, Jesus had declared, "Now is the judgment of this world and I, when I am lifted up from this earth, will draw all people to myself." The Gospel continues, "He said this to indicate the type of death he was to die" (12:31–33). We would like to see Pilate with the theatrical "thumbs up, thumbs down" gesture, but in John, what is up is down and what is down is up. The "lifting up" (12:32,34; 3:14; 8:28) becomes God's reversal of the debasement of the cross. The poison of the cross, like that of Moses' lifted serpent, becomes healing for those who really look upon it (Num 21:8–9). This deep looking pervades the passion story. The Paraclete will enable believers to look and judge in the same manner (16:8).

Seated in judgment, Pilate utters the third "looking" statement, "Behold your King." But the crowd only continues to shout, "Crucify him." Pilate then repeats to them, "Shall I crucify your King?" The chief priests as puppets of Rome reply, "We have no king but Caesar." Pilate will not contradict this and hands Jesus over to be crucified. Here we have a specific contrast between Jesus as king and the Roman emperor. This comes out clearly when we note that this is the third statement of "your king" in the Gospel. The first is on Palm Sunday when Jesus comes into Jerusalem on a donkey to fulfill the prophecy of Zechariah (9:9). In that text, the prophet describes a humble king on a donkey in contrast to the attitude of conquering kings on their great war horses. In contrast, the humble king will bring peace to the world (Zech 9:10).

This theme of peace and nonviolence appears again after Pilate's opening question to Jesus, "Are you the King of the Jews?" Jesus explains that he is not a king in the way Pilate thinks. He responds, "My kingdom is not from this world. If my kingdom were from this world, my followers would fight to keep me from being handed over to the Jews" (18:36). At his arrest, Jesus had restrained Peter from further resistance: "Put your sword back into its shield. Shall I not drink the cup that the Father has given me?" (18:11). The contrast between "no king but Caesar" and Jesus is between a king of military violence and a King of Peace.

After his condemnation, only in John's Gospel we have the statement that Jesus took the cross and carried it himself (19:17). In the other gospels, the soldiers force a certain Simon to carry it. This is a deliberate transition in John's Gospel. The cross is the great instrument of Roman domination, power, and superiority, but Jesus takes it as his own. He will triumph through the humiliation of the cross. Following this we have the next deeper meaning "seeing" text in regard to the handwritten inscription on the cross.

The Handwriting on the Cross: Jesus of Nazareth (Is) King of the Jews vs. "We Have No King but Caesar."

This is a "seeing" text because the cross is deliberately set up in a public place near the entry to Jerusalem and many passersby read the inscription. If we compare the description of the title in this Gospel with that in the others, we note significant differences. It is much longer and has a special message connected to it. In comparison with the inscription in the Synoptics, which are statements, this title is a faith proclamation, that Jesus the Nazorean is King of the Jews. The chief priests are alert to this and ask that it be changed to read, "This man said, I am King of the Jews" (19:21). However, Pilate, previously so vacillating, stands firm with the famous reply, "What I have written, I have written."

In all of this, Pilate is really acting as God's instrument. Previously, we have noted that Jesus told Pilate that he would have no power except it were given him from above. The idea that a mysterious divine power can be working beneath human words or events is also found in the story of Caiaphas the high priest. In plotting with others for the death of Jesus, he had stated that it was best that one man die for the people rather than having the nation destroyed (11:50). However, the evangelist notes immediately that Caiaphas, since he was high priest, had unwittingly prophesied that Jesus was to die not only for the nation but to gather together the scattered people of God. For added emphasis, this is later repeated in 18:14.

Pilate's refusal to change is an indication of the divine hand at work. The cross inscription is really God's proclamation and revelation of Jesus as King. The words, "What I have written," occur only once in the most important place in the Hebrew Bible. On Mount Sinai, after the blood covenant, God says to Moses, "I will give you the tablets of stone, *which I have written*" (Exod 24:12). It is also mentioned later that the two tablets of stone were written by the finger of God (31:18; 32:16). The idea of God's mysterious handwriting is also found in Daniel, where a mysterious hand appears on the wall and reveals God's plan to depose the king of Babylon (5:5, 24). So the writer is telling us that the cross title is really God's own handwriting and decree. Answering Jesus' statement about kingship, Pilate asked, "What is the truth?" He now answers his own question. The truth is not in Caesar's title but in God's new proclamation and unchangeable covenant through the cross.

Further details also enhance the mysterious meaning of the cross. The title is written in three languages to show Roman supremacy over the world reaffirmed through the victory on the cross. However, in view of Caiaphas's statement, it proclaims that Jesus died for the world, to bring together the scattered children of God (11:51). Other symbolism is also at work. The soldiers, too, according to the scriptures, divide Jesus' garments into four parts. The biblical number four often has a universal symbolism.

Matthew 24:31 describes the four winds in this manner. Special attention goes to the seamless tunic, closest to Jesus' body. The soldiers do not wish to tear it but cast lots for it. Biblical lots are often a way to leave things open to divine intervention. Oneness, despite universality and diversity, is a frequent Gospel theme, for example, "One flock and one shepherd" through gathering other sheep not of this fold (10:16). "One for the many" emerges from Caiaphas's prophecy that Jesus was to die not only for the nation but to gather the dispersed children of God. This universal oneness through gathering, invitation, and call is opposite to the violent Pax Romana imposed by the Roman military.

Jesus Becomes Universal King of Peace on the Cross

Standing by the Cross: Past or Present or Both?

> Standing by the cross of Jesus were his mother, and his mother's sister, Mary the wife of Clopas, and Mary Magdalene. When Jesus saw his mother and the disciple whom he loved standing beside her, he said to his mother, "Woman, here [literally, see] is your son." Then he said to the disciple, "Here [see] is your mother." And from that hour the disciple took her into his own home. (19:25–27)

Here we find three "seeing" statements inviting the Gospel audience to look for a deeper meaning. "Standing by" means much more, as in English at times, than merely being there. It means conformity and participation. The ultimate fear of any audience is death itself, which is a logical consequence of following Jesus. Yet, "the disciple whom Jesus loved" transcends any historical personage and stands for believers at any time. With the words, "Mother, see your son," they are invited to be part of Jesus' permanent family and successors. Yet how can this be? Jesus' mother, for example, has been dead for many years by the time this Gospel is written. Jesus has already provided the answer in advance with his promise, "Those who love their life will lose it, and those who hate their life in this world will keep it for eternal life. Whoever serves me must follow me, and where I am there will my servant be also" (12:25–26).

This eternal life is a key teaching of this Gospel, appearing eighteen times. To really follow Jesus one must be freed from the power of death. This is the ultimate freedom and peace. However, to follow Jesus and share this eternal life, it is necessary for him to first prove he has it himself. Previously he promised, "I lay down my life and take it up again. No one takes it from me. I have the power to lay it down and the power to take it up" (19:18). Only Jesus can say this because in John's Gospel he is the embodiment of the eternal Word of God: "In the beginning was the Word...and the Word became flesh" (1:1, 14). The way that Jesus dies must then be in his control and not in the ultimate power of death:

> After this, when Jesus knew that all was now finished, he said (in order to fulfill the scripture), "I am thirsty." A jar full of sour wine was standing there. So they put a sponge full of the wine on a branch of hyssop and held it to his mouth. When Jesus had received the wine, he said, "It is finished." Then he bowed his head and gave up his spirit. (19:28–30)

This story of Jesus' actual death is brief but very meaningful. The same Greek root, *tele*, is used three times for "finish" or "fulfill." Literally, it would be better translated "completed." In other words, his life is not untimely, but deliberately, completed as the incarnate Word of God on earth. One of the root meanings of "peace" is wholeness or completion. This is a favorite theme in John. During the Samaritan woman episode, Jesus states that his food is to do the will of his Father and complete his work (4:34). Later he speaks of the works that his Father has given him to complete (5:36). In Jesus' last prayer before his passion, he tells his Father that he has glorified him by completing the work he has been given to do (17:4). When he cured a lame man on the Sabbath, he stated that his purpose was to make a whole man well (7:23).

So Jesus deliberately dies when all is complete, for he had promised he would lay down his life and take it up again (10:18).

This tells the audience that for those who risk standing by the cross there can be no untimely death if they are joined to this Jesus. His expiration has a double meaning in what appears as a deliberate action: "He bowed his head and gave up [or handed over] his spirit." Later this will be symbolized after the resurrection when he breathes his Spirit into his disciples (20:22).

The Final Seeing: The Piercing of Jesus' Side and the Fountain of Water and Blood (19:31-37)

The preparation day for Passover was drawing to its close at sunset. So the Jewish authorities asked for Pilate's permission to break the legs of Jesus and the two other crucified men to hasten their death and removal from the crosses for burial. When they came to Jesus, they saw he was already dead, but one of the soldiers pierced his side with a lance, causing water and blood to issue forth. This final spear thrust was actually his worst wound because it was a desecration and mutilation of his dead body in sight of his family, beloved disciple, and friends who were looking on. It was a public disgrace before the world.

However, the beloved disciple, "the one who saw" the blood and water, discovered a deeper meaning and testified so others also might know the truth of the cross. This special meaning is found in the two scripture references at the end of the story of Jesus' death (19:36–37). The first is "None of his bones shall be broken." This is taken from the directions for preparing the paschal lamb meal (Exod 12:46). So the symbolism of the blood from Jesus' side points to understanding him in terms of the Passover. The background of this feast is from the time the Jews in Egypt were threatened by a deadly plague. To free his people from that threat, God told them to offer a lamb in sacrifice for each family. Then they were to take some of its blood and sprinkle it on the doors of their homes for healing and protection. God said, "This blood shall be a sign for you on the houses where you live. When I see the blood I will pass over you and no plague shall destroy you" (Exod 12:13).

At the foot of the cross, the beloved disciple saw this flowing blood as a sign that Jesus was the Passover Lamb who would save his people. The fact that it was flowing blood meant that it was the blood of sacrifice, since blood flowing to the ground was a ritual requirement. In the first pages of the Gospel, the Baptist had foretold that Jesus would be this Paschal Lamb with a double reference to seeing in a deeper manner. He saw Jesus coming to him and declared, "Here is [see] the Lamb of God who takes away the sin of the world." Beginning and end of the Gospel come together as the beloved disciple at the cross also sees Jesus as the Passover Lamb.

The liturgy at the Agnus Dei emphasizes the forgiving nature of this Lamb with the double acclamation, "Lamb of God who takes away the sin of the world, have mercy on us," and finally the added petition, "Grant us peace." The "sin of the world" is the lack of openness, or the darkness resulting from not relating to (or believing in) the Word/Light finally manifest in Jesus. In this forgiveness is found the ultimate meaning of peace as an interrelated wholeness and harmony with God as creator of the universe.

The second part of the sign, the flowing water, signifies the gift of the Spirit promised by Jesus, adding to forgiveness the quality of everlasting life. The whole Gospel points to this. First came Jesus' promise about himself and the Temple. At the first Gospel Passover Jesus had declared, "Destroy this temple, and in three days I will raise it up" (2:19). However, the author explains, "He [Jesus] was speaking of the temple of his body." So water coming from his body signifies water coming from the Temple in Jerusalem as God's special abode. Second, Jesus promised the Samaritan woman he would give her living water (4:10, 12).

Third, at the feast of Tabernacles, Jesus proclaimed in the Temple, "Let anyone who is thirsty come to me and let the one who believes in me drink" (7:37). Then he added that from within him will flow rivers of living water. The writer explains this as the Spirit that believers were to receive when Jesus would be glorified. Finally, we have the fulfillment of scriptures. Several texts describe water coming from the Jerusalem Temple in the last times. However, only in Zechariah do we find living water: "On that day living waters shall flow out from Jerusalem, half of them to the eastern sea and half of them to the western sea; it shall continue in summer as in winter" (14:8). This water symbolizes everlasting life for the text notes that the water never ceases to flow; it continues "summer as in winter," unlike most streams in Israel. Also, the water reaches the whole area from the eastern sea (the Dead Sea) to the western sea, the Mediterranean; this signifies a universal outreach. This parallels the universal meaning of the three languages on the cross inscription and the four divided parts of Jesus' garments.

The Inner Love Motivation Behind the Blood and Water

Jesus had stated this motive in his last words before the passion story, "That the love with which you [Father] have loved me may be in them and I in them" (17:26). This mutual shared love is a central Gospel theme. It is firmly embodied in the final "looking": "They will look upon the one whom they have pierced." In the passion account, the evangelist has focused on the piercing action (crucifixion, the nails, the wounds). The reaction to these wounds illustrates God's love: So this "looking" is followed by the reactions in the next verse in Zechariah: "They shall mourn for him as for an only child, and weep bitterly as for a firstborn" (12:10). This verse is also cited in "looking on" in the Book of Revelation (1:7). The audience is also invited to look on the one who is pierced. As a result, all the earth shall mourn.

In this "mourning as for an only child," the evangelist finds the most prominent biblical image of God's love, one derived from his highest attribute revealed to Moses, his *rachum* (Exod 34:6), based on *rechem*, the womb. This is because a mother's womb is the beginning locus of God's loving action. This is beautifully illustrated in Isaiah by God's words: "Can a woman forget her nursing child, or show no compassion for the child of her womb? Even these may forget, yet I will not forget you" (49:15). The verb *show compassion* is from *racham*, the same root as *rachum*. The beloved disciple deeply sensed this in Jesus' mother as he stood by her side. Words fail in this most emotional scene in the entire Bible. Artists have tried to capture it, especially in Michelangelo's Pietà; musicians, in the *Stabat Mater*.

The previous "looking" tableau, "Woman, behold your son" and "Behold your mother," now takes on deeper meaning: Jesus saw his mother and the disciple whom he loved, standing beside her at the cross. He said to his mother literally, "See your son," and then to the disciple, "See your mother." This disciple goes beyond any historical figure. It is any disciple whom Jesus loves as illustrated by Lazarus, "the one whom you love" (11:3) and the statement, "Jesus loved Martha and Mary" (11:5). The scene also transcends time when any believer contemplates the permanent mystery of the cross.

Jesus' actual mother had died many years before the writing of this Gospel. Yet she is alive and always present by the cross. The statements of Jesus show that he wants any believer at any time to take his place, along with Mary, into his permanent family. This includes much more than substitution or succession. It is a testament or heritage of deepest love. The beloved disciple has learned the *rachum* of God from how Jesus' mother looks upon the piercing of her son. He especially takes this love also to himself (to his home), as representing believers.

The ending of the passion story parallels the prologue conclusion on seeing: "No one has at any time seen God, the only child *[monogenēs]* in the Father's bosom has revealed him." *In the bosom* is a very affectionate term in the scriptures. The beloved disciple will parallel Jesus' relation to the Father. The writer describes him reclining at Jesus' bosom as a successor at the Last Supper. There Jesus reveals to him his great secret that Judas is about to betray him (13:25–26). This will start the process toward his death and the ultimate revelation of his love. This is brought out in the opening statement of the Last Supper when the evangelist writes that Jesus knew his hour was at hand to depart for the Father. This meant that "having loved his disciples who were in the world, he loved them to the end" (13:1).

The Enthronement Scriptural Text on Jesus as King of Peace

The image of the messianic king pouring out the living water, the promised Spirit, from the cross leads to the eschatological conclusion in Zechariah 4:10. This immediately follows the description of the living water flowing from Jerusalem in the last times. The text reads, "And the LORD will become king over all the earth; on that day the LORD will be one and his name one." It is universal because Zechariah describes all the nations of the world coming up to Jerusalem to join Israel in the worship of one God. "The LORD is one" in accord with the daily traditional Jewish prayer, the Shema, which begins with the words literally, "Hear, O Israel, the LORD is our God, the LORD is one" (Deut 6:4). So the declaration of God in Zechariah is a true image of a king of peace: that of one king and one worship of God combined with the diversity of many nations. Thus Jesus, in accord with the cross description, is truly a king of peace in contrast with Rome's military Pax Romana.

In regard to Zechariah, chapter fourteen with its description of the last times, living water, and the king of peace was an ancient reading for the great popular feast of Tabernacles, one of the three for which every Jew was obliged to celebrate by coming to Jerusalem. Zechariah 14:16 specifically mentions that all the nations would come to Jerusalem for the feast of Tabernacles, so this would assure a reading at the feast. We also see that Jesus went to the feast of Tabernacles. At the last great day of the festivity, he announced the gift of living waters to those who believed in him (7:38). The most likely reference is to Zechariah 12:8, for this is the only scripture text describing specifically living water coming from Jerusalem or the Temple.

King, Peace, and People in Preceding Texts

In the beginning of this chapter, we noted that we needed to start at the cross as a central focus of understanding. Now we can go further to show how the previous part of the Gospel leads to the cross, prepares for it, and even completes its meaning. As one guide for this journey we can take Moses, for Jesus himself had declared that if people believed in Moses, they would believe in him (Jesus) "for he wrote about me" (5:46). Jesus had in mind Moses' promise that God would raise up for them "a prophet like me from among the people" (Deut 18:15).

John's Gospel has twelve references to Moses, beginning right from the prologue. However, there are a number that receive special notice. Here the author may be following an old Christian tradition cited by St. Paul. He notes that our ancestors (Israel) were all baptized into Moses in the cloud (this was the bright cloud that showed them the way through the desert) and in the sea through which they all passed (it opened before them). All ate the same spiritual food (the manna in the wilderness) and all drank the same spiritual drink. "For they drank from the spiritual rock that followed them and the rock was Christ" (1 Cor 10:1-4). In three of these occasions—baptism, the manna in the wilderness, and the water from the rock—we find mention of "the Prophet" in the corresponding events of Jesus' life in the fourth Gospel. The first of these, baptism, centers around John the Baptist.

The Prophecy of John the Baptist on the Prophet and King

An official delegation of priests and Levites comes down from Jerusalem and asks John whether he is the Messiah, Elijah, or the Prophet. When the Baptist denies this, they ask him on what authority he baptizes since he is none of these (1:25). In return, John replies that he only baptizes with water but that Jesus, the one who came before him, yet after him is to baptize with the Holy Spirit. In regard to this, God gave the Baptist a sign to recognize him: It is the one upon whom he sees the Spirit as a dove descending and remaining on him. John declares, "I myself have seen and have testified that this is the Chosen One of God" (1:34). "Chosen One of God" is perhaps a better Greek manuscript reading than "Son of God." This title of "God's chosen one" is a special one that the Bible gives to certain kings, especially David, who are chosen by God through a special sign.

David's choice by God would be continued in his offspring as future kings. The audience would make this connection to God's word to Isaiah about a future kingdom of peace: "A shoot shall come out of Jesse [David's father] and a branch shall grow out of his roots. The Spirit of the LORD shall rest on him" (11:1–2). The mention that it would rest upon him is a likely link to the Baptist's revelation that the Spirit would come upon Jesus and remain upon him (1:32, 33). In regard to David, after he was anointed, the text reads that the Spirit came upon him from that day onward (1 Sam 16:13). The Baptist's designation of Jesus' as the Chosen One is paralleled by Nathaniel in the last of the series of titles used by disciples. Nathaniel declared to Jesus, "You are the Son of God! You are the king of Israel!" (1:49). "King of Israel" was a title adopted by David (2 Sam 6:20) as well as other kings.

In Isaiah, the prophet continues by describing the future kingdom of David as one of universal peace. Harmony and peace are symbolized in the animal world where ordinarily wild animals lie together and even a little child can play near a dangerous snake without harm (11:6–8). This peace spreads to the whole world, for the prophet declares that the earth will be filled with the knowledge of the Lord just as the waters of the sea cover the earth (11:9). This "Chosen One" title is linked to the cross where only God's handwriting proclaims that Jesus is the chosen king of the Jews. It is not something he takes upon himself. The Judean authorities had accused him literally of making himself a king (19:12). Jesus, however, tells Pilate that he was born a king: "For this I was born and came into this world, to testify to the truth" (18:37).

Jesus' Rejection of Violent Military Kingship After the Loaves Miracle

After the people had seen this sign they began to say, "This is truly the prophet who is to come into the world (6:14). This is a second "prophet" text in John according to God's promise to Moses in Deut 18:18, "I will raise up another prophet like you." Being like Moses would include bringing bread to the people, like the manna in the desert, as in the discourse that follows the miracle (6:31–32). And, of course, Moses was a military leader as well. But when Jesus realized the people were going to come and try to make him a king by force, he withdrew alone to the mountain (6:15).

No one can make Jesus a king nor has he tried to make himself one, as we have seen in the end of the previous section. In addition, Jesus is rejecting any kind of militant Messiah role. We have previously seen that he replies to Pilate that his kingship is not one of this world, where kings rely on violence and force. In the following loaves instruction, Jesus will provide true food, nourishment, and life for his people, not suffering and death as a military leader like Caesar.

The Palm Sunday Acclamation of Jesus as King of Peace (12:12–16)

This event receives more attention in John than in any other gospel. It is the second of only three occasions when the writer specifically states that after the resurrection, Jesus' disciples remembered the scriptures and understood them. The first concerns the meaning of the Jesus' mysterious saying about destroying the Temple and in three days raising it up (2:19–22). The third occurs after Peter and John visit the empty tomb (20:9). The differences in the story from the Synoptic accounts illustrate the special features in John.

In the Synoptics, Jesus' disciples, at his bidding, arrange to find a donkey and start the procession to Jerusalem. In John, it is the great Passover crowds at Jerusalem who hear Jesus is coming and go out to meet and welcome him. Then Jesus himself finds the donkey in order to fulfill the scriptures. In the other three gospels the crowds bless the one who comes in the name of the Lord. Only John adds to this, "The king of Israel." This is in addition to the mention in the prophecy of Zechariah, "Lo, your king comes to you, sitting on a donkey's colt." So we have a double mention of "your king." The details of the Zechariah prophecy (9:9–10) would be known to the audience: The victorious and triumphant king enters not in a proud manner but humbly upon a donkey. He destroys the attackers' military machines of chariots and war horses and he establishes peace among the nations. The image, then, is that of a true universal king of peace.

Jesus' Farewell Banquet and Testament of Peace (13—17)

Farewells in Jewish custom were always accompanied by greetings or best wishes of peace. The whole Last Supper has this peace atmosphere as a final farewell. The writer starts by writing that the Passover was near and that Jesus knew the hour had come for him to depart from this world and return to the Father. Jesus wishes to show them his love right to the end. This is despite his knowledge that even Judas, one of his trusted Twelve, was about to betray him (13:1–2). As a dramatic gesture of his love right to the end, Jesus rises from the table, casts aside his outer garments, and begins to wash his disciples' feet.

Washing a guest's feet was a traditional sign of welcome into the family circle where protection was assured and communion enjoyed. So peace, in its basic meaning of communion, was the ultimate object. However, to have protection and communion, some obstacles may need to be overcome. This could be previous enmity or lack of forgiveness or acceptance. Therefore the washing reached into the whole matter of personal relationships and forgiveness. The welcome had to be made by the household head. However, this was often delegated to someone of a lower rank at those times. This could be a woman or even a disciple or slave.

Jesus is a teacher, one who has come from God and has the highest rank. Yet he lays aside his garments of rank and performs this action as if he were a slave. His action is really a summary image of his whole life. He had come down from God to serve others with love and humility even to the extent of dying on the cross. Peter at first does not understand this and protests, "Lord, are *you* going to wash *my* feet?" (The italics show the emphasis in the Greek). Jesus insists that Peter does not understand what is happening but will know later. Then Peter repeats more emphatically, "You will never wash my feet"(13:9). Jesus finally declares that Peter will have no part with him if he does not have his feet washed. Only then does Peter tell Jesus to wash not only his feet, but his hands and head also. This whole dialogue illustrates Peter's later reluctance to follow Jesus as far as the cross in his love. His conversion or "turn around" will only come in chapter 21 when Jesus predicts how Peter will die to illustrate his love for Jesus' sheep.

This washing symbolism does not come out very well in a liturgy where feet have been thoroughly scrubbed and cleaned beforehand. In the writer's mind, the feet might be coated with mud, manure, or garbage before coming to the threshold of the house. Likewise, the process of forgiving may entail the removal of much "dirt." Jesus hints at this when he announces Judas' betrayal and predicts to Peter that he will deny him three times.

What Jesus does is once and for all, for the sins of the world. However, his disciples are to continue it by washing the feet of one another in the same spirit as Jesus:

> After he had washed their feet, had put on his robe, and had returned to the table, he said to them, "Do you know what I have done to you? You call me Teacher and Lord—and you are right, for that is what I am. So if I, your Lord and Teacher, have washed your feet, you also ought to wash one another's feet. For I have set you an example, that you also should do as I have done to you." (13:12–15)

"Peace I Leave with You"—The Full Meaning of Jesus' Peace in Contrast to Pax Romana

"Peace I leave with you; my peace I give to you. I do not give to you as the world gives" (14:27). Here we see a statement contrasting Jesus' peace with that of the world. To understand this difference we need to look at the context. Immediately afterward, Jesus says, "Do not let your hearts be troubled, and do not let them be afraid." This is a repetition of the same words as the opening ones in 14:1. There they immediately follow Jesus' sorrowful prediction that Peter, his closest apostle, will deny him not once but three times, even after protesting that he would be willing to lay down his life for him. This is what causes the troubled and fearful hearts. The same word, *troubled*, is used of Jesus when he announces for the first time that another apostle (Judas) will betray him: "Jesus was troubled in spirit" and announced that one of them would betray him (13:21).

So we need a closer look at what happened to Judas and Peter. First of all, let us look at Judas. The chief priests and Pharisees had sent out word that if anyone knew where Jesus was they should let them know so they might arrest him (11:57). The chief priests were the legitimate authority under Rome, so Judas decided to turn informer for his own security and advantage.

Some hint of his self-concern is in the next story about Mary's anointing of Jesus. Judas administered the community purse and objected that the ointment could have been sold for three hundred denarii and given to the poor (12:6). He was entrusted with such matters. At the Last Supper, when he went out to betray Jesus, some thought he was leaving to give something to the poor (13:29). With his plans to leave the group, a fatter purse would have been helpful.

An arrest of this nature would immediately command a response of Rome, so John's Gospel has a contingent of Roman soldiers accompany the Judean police to arrest Jesus at night (18:2–3). For the Romans, the capture and execution of potential threats to their government was a matter of maintaining security, which they called Pax Romana. So Judas decides to comply with their designs and obey their authority. This is the surest and safest way for him. An alliance with power and security could bring him many rewards. The way of Jesus may have been admirable for him, an ideal that he once had, but now it was simply too risky and unrewarding. Judas accompanied those arresting Jesus and literally "stood with them" (18:5).

Peter is quite different. While Judas appears more calculating, Peter seems more impetuous. At the Last Supper he declares before everyone that he is willing to lay down his life for Jesus (13:37). When the soldiers attempted to arrest Jesus, Peter courageously drew his sword and tried to defend his master. Later, when the police brought Jesus into the courtyard of the high priest, Peter was standing outside. However, the beloved disciple, who was known to the high priest, managed to have him brought in.

The woman gatekeeper asked Peter if he was one of Jesus' disciples. Then he began to vacillate and answered definitely, "I am not." Next he pretended to be among the police and attendants of the high priest, warming himself at a fire. The text notes incisively, "he was with *them*" (18:18). The author then deliberately repeats that he was standing and warming himself. This hints that he was getting "cold feet." This play on words was known at those times. Matthew notes that "the love of many will grow cold" (24:12). Then facing the same question before a questioning group, Peter replies again, "I am not." Finally an eyewitness who saw Peter striking his relative with a sword testifies against him. This was very serious. Peter immediately denied it and at that moment the cock crowed in fulfillment of Jesus' prophecy (13:38).

From these two examples we can find some characteristics of Pax Romana: It means compliance with government power and authority. Fear is its principal weapon, inducing people to look to them for security, safety, and other advantages. On the other hand, Pax Christi is based on Jesus' presence and relationship with him; it is his special gift: "My peace I give to you." The four chapters—14 to 17—are devoted to describing this relationship in many ways. Jesus' death will not mean an absence but a new and more powerful presence as Jesus sends the Paraclete, the Holy Spirit, to remain with them forever (14:15). This Spirit will be like a twin of Jesus, enabling the disciples to teach, bear witness, and do all the things that Jesus did with the same efficacy.

This presence will not be merely internal as opposed to the very visible Romans, who were behind all local government. It will manifest itself in a new visible solidarity dedicated to mirror Jesus' new love commandment to the world. This receives special focus in chapter 17, Jesus' final priestly and eternal prayer. There Jesus prays to his Father "that they may be one, as we are one" (11). This "oneness" is based on the loving union of Father and Son. It is opposed to the so called "unity" and conformity demanded by government authorities. We have previously seen that it is a oneness made possible by embracing diversity. Caiaphas had advised that one person die for the people, but the evangelist tells us that it is a one for the many, to gather together the dispersed children of God (11:52).

This word *one* is found five times in this chapter for special emphasis as Jesus repeatedly prays that the community will have this oneness. Twice, he states that this will be a supreme sign to the world that Jesus has sent them. The first reads, "That they may all be one. As you, Father, are in me and I am in you, may they also be [one] in us, so that the world may believe that you have sent me" (21). This oneness is particularly found in their love for one another. At the supper Jesus had said that his new commandment was "that you love one another as I have loved you" so that everyone would know they are his disciples (13:34–35). Now the concluding words of his prayer sum up his purpose: "That the love with which you [Father] have loved me may be in them and I in them" (26).

Peace and Overcoming the Powers of Darkness

In this fourth Gospel, peace has a cosmic origin in the harmony existing before creation: In the beginning was the creative Word of God, the source of all life and the light that came to being in all people (1:1–4). However, in the story found in the first chapters of Genesis, the ancestors of the human race revolted against this light. As a result darkness came about, and the disruption of the original peace and harmony. Yet despite this, the darkness did not overcome the light (1:5). This hints at the existence of an opposing force that has provoked failure in human beings. In late Old Testament literature and in the New Testament, the devil was considered the instigator behind human failure in the Garden of Eden. The Book of Wisdom notes, "Through the devil's envy, sin entered the world, and those who belong to his company experience it" (2:24). This becomes specific in John when Jesus addressed a group of Jewish believers as follows: "You are from your father the devil, and you choose to do your father's desires. He was a murderer from the beginning and does not stand in the truth, because there is no truth in him. When he lies, he speaks according to his own nature, for he is a liar and the father of lies" (8:43–44).

Jesus describes the devil as a murderer because he was the instigating cause of the death of the first parents. He is "from the beginning" as the Gospel starts, involved in the whole drama. He is also a liar because he deceived Adam and Eve with wrong information. As the Word, Jesus is also in conflict with him. Jesus' existence as the Word, going back in history, comes out in the next dialogue. This is introduced by Jesus' statement, "Amen, amen, I say to you, whoever keeps my word will never see death" (8:51).

The audience objects to this statement since Abraham and the prophets have died. Jesus replies, "Before Abraham was, I am *[ego eimi]*" (58). In John, these words function as part of the divine name revealed to Moses (Exod 3:14). This is recognized as blasphemous by the bystanders who pick up stones to cast at him. Later they will do the same when Jesus states that he and the Father are one (10:31). The *ego eimi* proclaims the existence of Jesus as eternal Word and thus taking part in conflict with Satan even in the Garden of Eden. Satan comes directly into the Gospel drama at the Last Supper when the writer notes that the devil had already suggested to Judas that he betray Jesus to the authorities (13:2). Judas makes his final decision when Jesus gives him a choice morsel at the supper: After he received it, "Satan entered into him" (13:27). Then Judas went out from the supper with the note, "And it was night"—a likely symbol of the devil and the powers of darkness.

The concern about the work of Judas, the devil, and the authorities continues in the discourses after the supper. Jesus tells his disciples, "The ruler *[archōn]* of this world is coming. He has no power over me" (14:30). This question about who has the superior power will be a central concern of the passion narrative. However, in anticipation, Jesus adds that his disciples will continue to bring Satan to judgment, because, "The ruler *[archōn]* of this world has already been judged" (16:30). This becomes a special concern in Jesus' last priestly intercession when he prays to his Father, "I ask you to protect them from the evil one." The references to the name of the Father and protecting them in that name (17:11–12) prepare the way for the conclusion: "I made your name known to them, and I will make it known, so that the love with which you have loved me may be in them, and I in them" (17:25).

In the following dramatic scene of Jesus' arrest, the superior power of that name will be made known. For the audience, the union of Satan, Judas, and Roman authorities warns the Gospel audience never to embrace the Roman confession. It also teaches them the need for higher powers if they are to resist that temptation. The place of Judas becomes real in those who denounce Christians to authority in the same way as Jesus was handed over (11:57). Peace and harmony in the world can never come until the ultimate cause of darkness is overcome.

The Garden Arrest and Conflict with Judas, Satan, and Roman/Judean Authorities (18:1–14)

"Jesus went out with his disciples across the Kidron valley to a place where there was a garden, which he and his disciples entered. Now Judas, who betrayed him, also knew the place, because Jesus often met there with his disciples." The word *garden* in this sense is only found in John's Gospel. It serves as a connecting link between three garden scenes: the arrest, the burial (19:41), and the resurrection (cf. 20:15). In the Old Testament it is found principally in Genesis 2 and 3 (fourteen times). Ancient exegetes saw this parallel: Just as the devil won a victory over the first parents in the garden, so also he tries to overcome Jesus in the same way. Here he works through Judas and the leaders of the attacking party, who are allied with Satan and Judas. Already we have learned that Satan entered into Judas at the Last Supper (13:2, 27).

Only in John, there is a "cohort" of Roman soldiers with him. A cohort was ordinarily six hundred men under a tribune (12), the superior officer of a centurion, about a hundred men. The exaggerated numbers emphasize Roman power rather than an actual description. Jesus and his disciples must be able to overcome all the power of Rome. In the scenes with Pilate, Jesus will tell the governor that he has no power over him except that given from above (19:11). There is also a detachment of police sent by the Jewish leaders. These were ordinarily maintained to keep order in the Temple area. They symbolize the Judean opposition mentioned three times in the Gospel: the parents and the cured blind man (9:22, 34). Also, some believers among the authorities did not confess this openly "for fear they would be put out of the synagogue" (12:42). In the discourse after the Last Supper, Jesus warns his disciples, "They will put you out of the synagogues" (16:1).

"Then Jesus, knowing all that was to happen to him, came forward and asked them, 'Whom are you looking for?'" (4) This knowledge of all about to happen (see also 13:1; 19:28) shows that everything is planned in advance as a summary of what will happen later in the crucifixion. It is really a previctory celebration of Jesus' passion and death. Jesus' advance forward to challenge the arresters illustrates his initiative—he is not a passive captive. In answer to their question, Jesus says, "I am," *ego eimi*. We have already seen this to be an expression of the powerful divine name of the Father that protects him as well as his disciples. Consequently, when the attackers heard this, "they stepped back and fell to the ground." It was customary to bow one's head in worship on hearing the divine name. Often, "falling down" accompanies this. In the psalms, God's enemies are described as falling back in submission.

Ego eimi is also an expression of inextinguishable divine life. We have seen that when Jesus said that those who keep his word would never see death, he confirms this by expressing his eternal existence, even before Abraham, by this *ego eimi*. Judas is again mentioned by name to show his solidarity and that of Satan with those behind the attempt to arrest Jesus. For greater emphasis, Jesus asks again whom they are seeking, followed by the same effects. In all, the *ego eimi* is repeated three times.

The author enhances the dramatic effect of the scene by having it take place in darkness with Judas and his band carrying lanterns and torches. Previously the text had noted that after Satan entered Judas, he went out from the supper and "It was night." The dim oil lamps and torches contrast with Jesus who is the light of the world. The scene is really an enactment of the prologue verse, "The light shines in darkness, and the darkness did not overcome it" (1:5). No demonic or earthly power can arrest Jesus and cause his death unless he temporarily allows them to do so. As a result, Jesus finally answers, "I told you that I am he. So if you are looking for me, let these men go" (8). The author then notes, "This was to fulfill the word that he had spoken, 'I did not lose a single one of those whom you gave me'" (9). Jesus willingly offers his own life so the lives of his disciples may be saved from any fear of death. This has been previously stated in his final prayer in 17:12, as also in 6:39. In addition, he had promised that as a good shepherd, "I give them eternal life, and they will never perish. No one will snatch them out of my hand" (10:29). He follows this by the statement, "I and the Father are one." This occasioned a shower of stones from the crowd. What Jesus does is an act of obedience to his Father.

When Simon Peter begins a violent defense by effectively using his sword, Jesus tells him to put it back in its sheath and adds, "Am I not to drink the cup that the Father has given me?"

(18:11). After this, Jesus permits his arrest. In all, the arrest conflict sharply contrasts the powers behind the Roman confession and the Christian confession inscribed on the cross. It assures the audience that no authority can effectively arrest them as followers of Jesus. It also teaches that Jesus opposes the use of violence as opposite to the message of peace he is bringing to the people as a nonviolent Messiah of Peace. As such, he and his followers will overcome the violent military power of Rome. At his last discourse, he told his disciples to have confidence in victory. In his last words before his final prayer, he said that he had told them these things "so that in me you may have peace." This is despite the persecution and suffering they will face. "But take courage, I have conquered the world" (16:33).

The Resurrection Stories, Jesus' Final Triple Greeting of Peace, and Last Blessing

The peaceful garden images linger. They are twice noted at Jesus' burial and then again in Mary Magdalene's visit to the tomb. There she first thinks that the risen Jesus might be the gardener (20:15). Mary Magdalene is the first one to meet the risen Jesus. He gives her the special commission to bring the good news to other disciples. They had gathered together behind locked doors out of fear of the Jewish authorities who might hand them over to Pilate like Jesus for crucifixion. Jesus greets them for the first time, "Peace be with you" (20:19), and then shows them his hands and his side. This indicates that he is indeed the crucified one come back to life. The disciples rejoice at this sight since they know that he has overcome death and its power as he promised: "I lay down my life in order to take it up again. No one takes it from me, but I lay it down of my own accord. I have power to lay it down, and I have power to take it up again" (10:17–18). Since he has done this for his disciples, their deep fear of Roman/Judean authorities can disappear in favor of inner peace and security. Roman power over life gives way to Jesus' power.

The second greeting of peace follows with the commission: "As the Father has sent me, so I send you." All that Jesus has done for his disciples will continue with the same power from the Father. This sending is dramatized in his next gesture: "He breathed on them and said to them, 'Receive the Holy Spirit.'" The promise of the sending of the Holy Spirit, the Paraclete, dominates the Last Supper discourse. The Paraclete will duplicate in the disciples all that Jesus was able to do. This Spirit will remain with them forever (14:16). Just as the Word/Wisdom became incarnate in Jesus, so also, by way of parallel, the Paraclete/Spirit becomes incarnate in the lives of Jesus' followers.

Of all that Jesus did, the delivery from sin and its power is primary. John the Baptist declared this in his first introduction of Jesus as the Lamb of God who takes away the sin of the world (1:29) and repeated often (8:21, 24; 9:41; 15:22–24; 16:8–9). It is the likely meaning of Jesus' humble and loving washing of the disciples' feet with its command that the disciples wash the feet of one another (13:1–20). So Jesus transfers this power with the words, "Whose sins you shall forgive are forgiven and whose sins you shall retain are retained." This is the essence of the inner peace that Jesus promised to leave them in the Last Supper discourses.

The third greeting of peace comes eight days later when the disciples are gathered together once more. At this time, Thomas makes his great confession, "My Lord and my God" (20:28). These were titles that Roman emperors either claimed or aspired to at the end of the first century. Domitian (AD 80–96), for example, was fond of the title of Lord and God. *Kyrios* was a title often given to gods in the East. Jesus has proved his possession of these titles by his victory over death. Now believers, calling on him as *Kyrios* and *Theos*, can have peace and lose their fear of any external power—especially that of the Roman military.

Thus the final three greetings of peace sum up the victory of the confessional cross inscription of Jesus as king of peace over every power of death, sin, or any external force. They proclaim an internal peace resulting from the presence of the risen Christ/Paraclete. Thus they differ from the Pax Romana forcibly imposed by the Roman military to control any opposition or dissent to Caesar. Believers need no longer fear the consequences of the refusal to confess, "We have no king but Caesar."

After these final peace greetings and empowerment, the risen Jesus blesses the Gospel audience with the words, "Blessed are those who have not seen and yet have believed." Then an earlier closing states the purpose of the Gospel. In the beginning, in the Word was *life* and now believing in Jesus' name, they may have *life* also (20:31).

Summary Points for Praxis, Teaching, and Ministry

In John's Gospel, a "beloved disciple" is one who stands beside the cross of Jesus with the peace and love it stands for. This contrasts with Judas the informer who "was standing" with government forces who arrested Jesus for disturbing the Pax Romana, which demanded submission and compliance. Judas was looking for his own security and advantage. For a time, Peter also, out of fear and cowardice was "standing" outside the high priest's courtyard, pretending to be one of the attendants and police rather than with Jesus. A favorite title of Caesar was "father of his country," *pater patriae*. This is the origin of the word *patriotism*. This false patriotism relied on keeping people in a permanent state of fear, offering them security, "peace," and protection from outside enemies, especially the "terrorists" of that day. In contrast, Pax Christi relies on love, relationship, and a spirit of daring to stand by the cross.

- Contemplation of the cross is the greatest source for learning the meaning of Christ's death. This is especially true for the teacher or preacher. The scene at the cross transcends history, past, present, and future. Thus the mother of Jesus is always there as the one who best understood and appreciated that "God so loved the world that he gave his only Son" (3:16). The beloved disciple forever remains at the side of Jesus' mother inviting us to meditate and contemplate the cross so we can drink from the fountain of the Spirit that comes from the side of the crucified Jesus.

- After the Last Supper, Jesus gave us his final will and testament in the words: "Peace I leave with you; my peace I give to you" and in contrast, "I do not give to you as the world gives" (14:27). Thus, Jesus is shalom as the title of this book bears. In this gift of himself, there is a deep relationship of trust. However, it is not just "my personal Jesus" in a purely individual sense. It manifests itself in a deep solidarity with other believers that becomes a concrete witness to the world, according to Jesus' final prayer to his Father: "I in them and you in me, that they may be completely one, so that the world may know that you sent me and have loved them even as you have loved me" (17:22).

BIBLIOGRAPHY

This is not meant to be a complete bibliography of sources but a selection of those most frequently used in writing this book.

Abbot, Walter M., ed. *The Documents of Vatican II.* New York: Guild Press, America Press, Association Press, 1966.

Allison, Dale C. *The Sermon on the Mount.* New York.: Crossroad, 1999.

Boadt, Lawrence. *Reading the Old Testament: An Introduction.* Mahwah, N.J.: Paulist Press, 1984.

Brown, Raymond E. *The Community of the Beloved Disciple.* Mahwah, N.J.: Paulist Press, 1979.

Byrne, Brendan. "Jesus as Messiah in the Gospel of Luke: Discerning a Pattern of Correction." *Catholic Biblical Quarterly* 65 (2003): 80–95.

Carter, Warren, in *Matthew's Parables* by Carter, Warren and Heil, John Paul. *Catholic Biblical Association Monograph Series* 30, CBA, 1998.

Cassidy, Richard J. *Jesus, Politics and Society: A Study of Luke's Gospel.* Maryknoll, N.Y.: Orbis, 1978.

Cassidy, Richard J., and Philip Scharper, eds. *Political Issues in Luke–Acts.* Maryknoll, N.Y.: Orbis, 1983.

Crosby, Michael J. *House of Disciples: Church, Economics and Justice in Matthew.* Maryknoll, N.Y.: Orbis, 1988.

Fiorenza, Elizabeth. *In Memory of Her.* New York: Crossroads, 1983.

Ford, J. Massyngbaerd. *My Enemy Is My Guest: Jesus and Non-Violence in Luke.* Maryknoll, N.Y.: Orbis, 1984.

Grassi, Joseph A. *The Hidden Heroes of the Gospel.* Collegeville, Minn.: Liturgical Press, 1989.

———. *Informing the Future: Social Justice and the New Testament.* Mahwah, N.J.: Paulist Press, 2003.

Johnson, Luke T. *The Literary Function of Possessions in Luke-Acts.* Atlanta, Ga.: John Knox, 1983.

Malina, Bruce. *The New Testament World: Insights from Cultural Anthropology.* Atlanta, Ga.: John Knox, 1981.

Murphy, Catherine M. *Wealth in the Dead Sea Scrolls & in the Qumran Community.* Leiden, Boston, Mass.: Brill, 2002.

Murphy-O'Connor, Jerome. *Paul: A Critical Life.* New York: Oxford University Press, 1996.

Neyrey, Jerome. *The Passion According to Luke.* Mahwah, N.J.: Paulist Press, 1985.

Nolan, Albert. *Jesus Before Christianity.* Maryknoll, N.Y.: Orbis, 2001.

Oakman, Douglas E. *Jesus and the Economic Questions of His Day.* Lewiston, N.Y.: Edwin Mellen Press, 1986.

Powell, Mark Allen. *What Are They Saying About Luke?* Mahwah, N.J.: Paulist Press, 1989.

Senior, Donald. "With 'Swords and Clubs'—The Setting of Mark's Community and His Critique of Abusive Power." *Biblical Theology Bulletin* 17 (1987): 10–20.

Topel, L. John. *Children of a Compassionate God: A Theological Exegesis of Luke 6:20–49.* Collegeville, Minn: Liturgical Press, 2001.